If advertising, marketing, media or consumers in one of the world's largest markets interest you, then this book is for you. It offers, in small readable snippets, a quick look at issues, brands and trends ranging from the Tata Nano to the attitude of marketers to media spends. I enjoyed reading it.

Vanita Kohli-Khandekar
Media specialist
Author, The Indian Media Business
and The Making of Star India

Chinta has a lot to offer in his book – blogs, articles and speeches that cover stories of iconic brands and companies; communication in all its manifestations; and the role of media houses. Particularly enjoyable are the insights that he has distilled over four decades of a varied and rich experience. As his client in Cadbury, I found his approach to advertising comprehensive and persuasive, the consequence of a mind that is curious, continually questioning and learning.

Vinita Bali
*Independent Director
Previously in leadership roles at
The Coca-Cola Company,
Cadbury Schweppes & Britannia*

As a media researcher I was especially drawn to Chinta's observations on media and its regulation. The themes cover, *inter alia*, the use (actually abuse) of statistics; issues of regulation (ownership, content and behaviour); sports broadcasting rights; and television audience measurement, on which we worked together consulting for TAM. In a fast changing media world these themes have a continuing relevance, and not only in India.

Ivor Millman
British Media and Market Researcher

In an industry where the urgent chronically tends to overshadow the important, *Take it from Me...* is a vibrant invitation to look beyond the events that jam the headlines, and focus on the underlying logic of them – to switch attention from the "who" and "what", to the "why"; "how" things connect and impact the business, and "where" they are driving it. For us to take action.

Read it cover-to-cover, or browse through it following your interests, to help develop and structure the very thing that's the fuel as well as the output of our profession: ideas.

Giovanni Fabris
Media consultant
Former VP, International Media at McDonald's
As chair of the WFA Media Committee,
co-author of the Global Guidelines
for TV Audience Measurement

Chintamani Rao, in his understated, quiet manner, provides a provocative perspective on many issues related to the marketing, advertising and media industries. Drawing from his rich experience in this business, he shares his wisdom which is both enriching and enjoyable. Written simply yet with much elegance, *Take it from Me...* is highly recommended to any practitioner in this business. His reflections on two towering personalities and seven life lessons are cherries on a well baked cake.

Madhukar Sabnavis
Vice Chairman, Ogilvy India

OCCASIONAL THOUGHTS ON
MARKETING AND MEDIA

TAKE IT FROM ME….

CHINTAMANI RAO

PARTRIDGE

Copyright © 2019 by Chintamani Rao.

ISBN:	Hardcover	978-1-5437-0584-3
	Softcover	978-1-5437-0583-6
	eBook	978-1-5437-0582-9

All rights reserved. No part of this book may be used or reproduced by any means, graphic, electronic, or mechanical, including photocopying, recording, taping or by any information storage retrieval system without the written permission of the author except in the case of brief quotations embodied in critical articles and reviews.

Because of the dynamic nature of the Internet, any web addresses or links contained in this book may have changed since publication and may no longer be valid. The views expressed in this work are solely those of the author and do not necessarily reflect the views of the publisher, and the publisher hereby disclaims any responsibility for them.

Print information available on the last page.

To order additional copies of this book, contact
Partridge India
000 800 10062 62
orders.india@partridgepublishing.com

www.partridgepublishing.com/india

CONTENTS

About this book ix

Marketing and Advertising

1. The End of the World as We Know It? 1
2. Back to the Future 6
3. Fall from Heaven..10
4. Marketing 101 at the Bottom of the Pyramid ...15
5. "I'm Too Sexy for my Shoes" 22
6. A Service is not a Product 26
7. Marketing is about People............................31
8. Leadership, The Old-Fashioned Way 36
9. It's not about the Elephant............................41
10. "You've Come a Long Way, Baby!"................. 46
11. The State of Marketing is Worrying...............51
12. Wanted: More Magic, Less Logic....................57
13. Crowdsourcing: No Safety in Numbers......... 63
14. Marketing Forgot Him – and That Shows 68

Media and Media Regulation

15. As Ye Sow... 75
16. "Everybody Has Won, and All Must Have Prizes."... 79
17. All News is Good News................................. 89
18. Mirror, Mirror, on the Wall.......................... 93
19. Politics, Theatrics, and the Economics of News.. 96
20. Media Ownership: More Questions than Answers..103

21 Can't Imagine What They Were Thinking.... 111
22 The TAM Has Come...................................... 115
23 Media Regulation: Between the Devil
and the Deep Sea 120
24 So Where should the Money Come From? ...128
25 The New TV Ratings System has
Drawbacks, Too 136
26 Like the Curate's Egg: Good in Parts 146
27 The Yogi and the Commissar 153
28 NBA vs Republic TV — the Pot Calling
the Kettle...? 170
29 Justice Delayed, but not Denied.................. 179
30 There are None so Blind as Those Who
Will Not See 187
31 One More for the DPOs 203
32 Why Sports Broadcasting is Becoming
a Lose-Lose Game 209

Managing

33 Remembering Mani Ayer 235
34 Accountability is a Two-Way Street 239
35 My Life, in Seven Lessons 246
36 A Man of Many Parts 254

ABOUT THIS BOOK

I have spent over forty stimulating years in two connected but distinct spaces: advertising, with a focus on brands and brand strategy; and the media, in which I have also had a great deal of involvement in policy and regulatory issues. What they have in common is that both are about mass communication, and creating content; and both are dependent on highly talented people.

Over the years, as an observer and a keen student of marketing and media, I have been writing articles from time to time on contemporary developments. This book is a compilation of a selection of those, ones that I believe have lasting relevance as they raise and address issues that continue to matter today. I have added contextual notes and updates where necessary.

As these pieces address quite a wide array of subjects, I have grouped them into three broad sections: Marketing and Advertising; Media and Media Regulation; and Managing, the last including tributes to two giants I had the great good fortune to work with. The pieces within each section are arranged in chronological order of writing.

MARKETING AND ADVERTISING

1

THE END OF THE WORLD AS WE KNOW IT?

> *"Future historians of our trade will be baffled. Towards the end of the 20th century, more and more marketing companies were converted to a belief in seamless, all-media, 360°, harmonised, orchestrated, integrated communications. And at exactly the same time, the purveyors of those communications disintegrated completely."*
>
> *-- Jeremy Bullmore, 'Who's going to sit at the client's top table?' AdMap, Oct 2004*

The 2010 Marketing Outlook report of The CMO Council is out, with mixed messages for advertising and media agencies.

At a time when they are coming out of a downturn, 58% of respondents "have no intention

---

[1] Blog post first published in April 2010

of switching agencies, and most rate the value and contributions of their agency partners as pretty good (35%) or extremely valuable (18%)".

That sounds good, except that they expect to reduce their dependence on traditional agencies, and work instead with distributed specialist shops.

At the top of the marketing agenda in 2010 are investing in digital demand generation and online relationship building; exploring alternative media and new routes to market; and crunching customer data to improve segmentation and targeting. It is precisely in these areas – of new technology and data analytics – that marketers find agencies most wanting.

In trouble ever since the media function was hived off from the advertising agency (which the agencies did to themselves), the traditional client-agency relationship model has been under further strain with the advent of new technologies and new media.

As the Internet increasingly became a force most agencies, versed in the crafts of traditional media, talked about it but did little. Some ignored it; others made some expedient arrangement, and added a couple of slides to their credentials presentation, trying to look future-ready. But mostly conversations about 'digital' or 'interactive' were between young account management and creative people and their marketing counterparts, who were active Internet users. Agency managements had little to do with the subject.

Meanwhile the beast kept growing, and spawned a new breed of creative people who talked like geeks and worked out of small shops with quirky names like Webchutney.

Two or three years ago I visited Microsoft, Yahoo and Google at their HQs, getting updated on the Internet. All three said they dealt directly with advertisers because advertising agencies just didn't get it: and they were talking not of India but of the US and of the world in general.

I thought they were a little unkind, but I was disabused of that idea just a few weeks later when John Dooner, then Chairman of McCann WorldGroup, came to India to launch McCann's 'Digital Initiative'. In a press interview at the time he said, "What are people getting from the Internet? Information, or exchanging emails. That's the primary use of the Internet. It certainly isn't social intercourse in the truest sense of the word. It's certainly not creating the smell of a newspaper."

And about mobile phones: "A mobile is what it is. I'm starting to get mobile messages, and it's terribly annoying.... I'm going to treat that more as a practical thing, something that would allow me to create an interaction or transaction."

No wonder the CMO Council says agencies are "struggling to evolve as marketing and traditional media go digital", resulting in a "power shift from master agency control of accounts to a more digitally empowered client wielding new partner and provider connections."

Agencies are specialists, or used to be, in understanding people: what makes them tick and how to move them to buy. It is not the technology inside the box that they need to know and understand: it is how people engage with the box and what communication potential it represents. Technology is only an enabler, and specialist skills in that area can be hired or outsourced, by client or agency.

Romancing with words and pictures instead of with their purpose, agencies have ceded ground to all manner of service providers. The latest pushback, on the final frontier, is Unilever's announcement last week of a global creative crowdsourcing initiative for a clutch of brands[2]. Looking to get entries from hundreds of filmmakers, Unilever is offering £70,000 in prizes – and what it saves on agency fees it intends to spend on buying media. Yet Unilever's spokesperson assures us this move 'does not

---

[2] See p. 63, *Crowdsourcing: no safety in numbers*

replace or interfere with our relationships with agencies'!

If this is the beginning of the end of the world as we know it, the agencies have, sadly, only themselves to blame. Bill Bernbach's words of warning come to mind: "We'll die in our marketplace. On our shelves. In our gleaming packages of empty promises. Not with a bang. Not with a whimper. But by our own skilled hands."

2

BACK TO THE FUTURE

When the CEO of the world's largest Media agency talks about the future of media planning, you'd better listen carefully. But when that promising future – predicated upon the evolution of technology – is what you were doing 15 years ago, you begin to wonder....

Interviewed at the IAA New York Global Marketing Summit, Irwin Gotlieb, CEO of Group M, was asked if there was something marketers should do differently. "We need to define new ways of targeting audiences," he said.

Elaborating, "He outlined how we are three to four years away from a level of granularity that may help marketers pinpoint when a consumer is planning a major purchase. For example, automakers may be able to better utilize existing data on a consumer's current vehicle make and model, along with the end date of a current lease

---

[1] Blog post first published in Apr 2010

or loan agreement, to offer specific messages in the 45 day period before that consumer plans to buy another car," reports Internationalist magazine.

That's all he hopes will be possible three or four years from now? Ogilvy in Jakarta was doing that more than 15 years ago, with neither depth of research nor even as much data processing capability as every college kid has today.

One of our clients in Jakarta was Toyota Astra Motor. Toyota's local partner Astra also owned Auto 2000, the largest auto retail chain in the country; Mobil 88, a used car dealership; and Astra Finance, a finance company that gave auto loans. Put this together, and what do you have?

Ogilvy handled Direct Marketing for the Toyota Corona. It was not hard to figure that our best prospects were satisfied Toyota Corolla upgraders. We knew the average replacement cycle was three years. Putting together all our client's data resources we identified those who had owned a Toyota Corolla for two years and more, and then here's what happened.

Against the backdrop of the on-going advertising of all the businesses, including for the new Toyota Corona, this Corolla owner received an invitation to test drive the new car. Meanwhile he also got a mailer from Mobil 88 telling him there was a good market for two- to three-year old Corollas, and inviting him to drive in for a free valuation. About the same time he got a mailer from Astra Finance, offering finance for the Toyota Corona on attractive terms.

So, in three seemingly independent, orchestrated pieces of targeted communication, the hot prospect was invited to experience the new car; offered assistance to buy it; and offered help to dispose of his old car. Loop closed.

When we worked this out there was no great flash of brilliance; there was no thunder and lightning: it just seemed like a good idea, even a clever little idea, and a lot of hard work ahead given the limited data processing capabilities of the time. I've no doubt that with premeditated data capture and better technology you could layer the whole campaign and separately target prospects having different levels of engagement with the brand. But that's only a matter of degree, not a new way of doing things.

More revelations follow: "[Gotlieb] believes that future marketing budgets will be bifurcated to just two disciplines. The first allocation will go to general awareness…. The second allocation will go to specifically targeted messages…"

"There is no question," the magazine continues, "that Group M's CEO sees a marketing world ahead that embraces both targeting and broad awareness...."

I don't want to believe that is all the head of the world's largest Media agency has to say about the future. Someone please tell me it's just bad reporting.

3

FALL FROM HEAVEN

"How art thou fallen from heaven, O Lucifer, son of the morning!"

-- Isaiah 14:12

Procter & Gamble is in a public-relations war with its consumers: angry blogging parents demanding that the company withdraw the new Pampers diapers, which they say are unsafe.

What started with one anguished mother creating a Facebook page, "RECALL PAMPERS DRY MAX DIAPERS!" grew into a tide of the so-called mommy bloggers and resulted last week in two class action lawsuits against P&G. The allegation is that Pampers Dry Max can cause severe rashes, blisters, chemical burns, infections and other ailments in babies who wear it, and that P&G knew that but let consumers take the risk.

---

[1] Blog post first published in May 2010

"The best you can do," as Anant Rangaswami said yesterday in his *Campaign India* blog, writing not about P&G but about the open online environment in general, "is to try and get into the conversation and engage with the aggrieved and smoothen ruffled feathers."

Procter & Gamble, global consumer packaged goods giant and long-time marketing school of the world, got into the conversation not to smoothen ruffled feathers but to confront the aggrieved: "These rumours are being perpetuated by a small number of parents, some of whom are unhappy that we replaced our older Cruisers and Swaddlers products while others support competitive products and the use of cloth diapers." So it's a conspiracy between P&G's competition and the cloth diaper lobby, and those are fake mothers on Facebook and Twitter?

In an interview with Bloomberg a P&G spokesman dismissed the whole thing as a storm in a teacup, when he said the company had received "one rash complaint for every 5 million Dry Max diapers sold – about 400 complaints so far."

"We're insulted that someone would imply that our products are dangerous," he said.

Insulted? That's an emotionally charged statement coming from a company. By using intemperate language P&G is giving away that it is not in control. That spokesman should be gagged.

This incident naturally brings to mind the time, nearly 30 years ago, when in three days seven unconnected people in the Chicago area died of cyanide poisoning, and it turned out each of them had taken Extra-Strength Tylenol. The scale of media coverage was unprecedented: according to one estimate, the story had the widest domestic media coverage of any since the assassination of President Kennedy; and an awareness study showed that over 90% of Americans knew about it within a week of the crisis.

That was in 1982, before the Internet, before this interconnected world we live in. But Johnson & Johnson did not dismiss it saying Tylenol was perfectly safe and that seven was a very small number relative to the number of Tylenol tablets sold.

Though it was conclusively established to the satisfaction of the authorities that the contamination had not taken place in J&J's facilities, the company took full responsibility for preventing further mishap. Far from denying, obfuscating, defending, or offering facile explanations, J&J came out in the open and took affirmative action. It recalled 31 million bottles of Tylenol at a cost to itself of $50 million;

and mounted a massive outreach programme to stop people from consuming any Tylenol they might have in stock at home.

Within ten weeks of the recall J&J started putting Extra-Strength Tylenol back on the shelves, in new tamper-resistant packaging. In time Tylenol, thought as good as dead, won back consumer confidence and 95% of the market share it had prior to the poisonings.

That is what trust is about. And great brands are built on trust, above all. The trouble starts when marketers take that trust lightly and their brands make promises they can't deliver, often justified as creative licence. But it's not what you say that counts; it's what the consumer gets out of it. And when someone trusts you they take it that you mean what you say.

Trust, and living up to it, doesn't mean mistakes and mishaps won't occur. But respecting that trust helps guide how you deal with that situation: as J&J did with Tylenol, or as P&G is with Pampers?

It doesn't matter whether the affected are many or a few; or whether their complaints are serious or trivial; or if they are the lunatic fringe. What matters is what millions of others see, read and hear and what, consequently, they feel about the company and the brand. Buyers of Pampers unaffected by the reported problems; users of

Tide, Crest, Whisper, Olay, and Gillette who faithfully buy these brands: they may just begin to wonder.

These things don't happen overnight. Trust built over generations doesn't crumble but it does erode and weaken, and takes less time to erode than it did to build. That's not difficult to imagine. Think of the trust between two people, and apply the same principle.

Far be it from me to preach about brands to P&G, who many would believe wrote not just the book but the holy book, but this does feel like your high priest has turned atheist.

4

MARKETING 101 AT THE BOTTOM OF THE PYRAMID

> *"We first reduce the price to a point where we believe more sales will result. Then we go ahead and try to make the price. We do not bother about the costs. The new price forces the costs down. The more usual way is to take the costs and then determine the price, [but] what earthly use is it to know the cost if it tells you that you cannot manufacture at a price at which the article can be sold? One may calculate what a cost is, [but] no one knows what a cost ought to be."*
>
> -- Henry Ford, *My Life and Work, 1923*

Whether hailed for inventing the assembly line or derided for famously offering the Model T in "any colour so long as it is black", Henry Ford

---

[1] First published in *The Smart Manager*, May-June 2010

is associated with manufacturing efficiency, rather than with why he did what he did.

Ford determined that the optimum price for the Model T was $500. He then set about managing the cost so that it could be sold profitably at that price. The assembly line was one outcome of that process; limiting the colour to black was another.

Western analysts looking today at innovations coming out of emerging market economies and derisively dismissing them as "modern versions of the Model T Ford" don't know how right they are, because what they is see a stripped-down product, not the reason why it was built (not stripped-down) that way.

That they are caught in the web of their own thinking is evident from patronizing terms like "frugal innovation" and "de-engineering" to describe product innovations coming especially out of India and China. *The Economist*, in a gushing special report on innovation in emerging markets, cynically says, "People in the West like to believe that their companies cook up new ideas in their laboratories at home and then export them to the developing world, which makes it easier to accept job losses in manufacturing."

Innovation is about people

Innovation has long been thought to be a technological breakthrough embodied in a new product that is adopted by the elite and trickles down to the masses – or which the masses ooze up to – over time. That is born of inside-out thinking, of techies making new products technically superior to existing ones.

In fact, innovation today is about making it possible for a larger number of people to enjoy the benefits that products bring. The distinction is critical, because people don't buy products; they buy the expectation of benefits. No one actually needs a refrigerator, for example: they need to be able to cool water and preserve food. If you can help them do that without electricity or without the use of Freon gas, even they can't make ice in it they won't complain. (You should still call it a refrigerator, because that word instantly conveys what the product does: that's communication.)

Innovation, then, must focus on people, not on technology; not just on products that do things better but on products that enable a larger number of people to do things with greater efficiency or greater convenience, or in greater safety and comfort.

It was out of such thinking that in the 1970's Nirma was born. Far from a technological advance, it was technological regression. But what it did was to bring to millions of women in India the soak-and-rinse efficiency and convenience of a bucket wash instead of labouring with a bar of laundry soap. Exposed to the advertising of Surf, these women were aware of detergent powder but found it far too expensive. So they did not have to be sold the idea of the product, simply to be given a product they found affordable.

It took Hindustan (Uni)Lever some 15 years to find a way to compete with Nirma. And they got it right when they started with the price, not with the product. After several false starts Lever finally asked themselves the right question: how to make a detergent powder that could be profitably marketed at Rs 7/- per kg. The result was Wheel, HUL's largest brand today. Far from being a stripped-down ('de-engineered') product, it was built bottom-up. More, it was not simply a cost-effective product formulation; it was a whole manufacturing and business system born out of re-thinking.

Nirma and Wheel have gone so deep into history now that they are not even talked about in today's Nano world. Speaking of which, the Tata Nano is actually the new Model T Ford, starting as it did with quite the same intention: of making a car that could be sold at a pre-determined price. And that is not de-engineering or re-engineering: it is re-thinking.

Nor is innovation only about price: it is about enabling. At the heart of the amazing growth of mobile telephony in India from zero to 600 million connections in 15 years is the pre-paid facility. It recognizes that in India the number of people who can deal with a monthly billing cycle is relatively small: the large majority of potential (now actual!) users either don't have a monthly earning cycle – your carpenter, plumber, *dhobi, bhajiwala, kabadi* – or otherwise need to exercise tight control on spending, and can put out small sums of money as and when they have it. (Also perhaps, before security regulations kicked in, that there was a large number of big spenders who wanted not to leave a paper trail.)

The pre-paid mobile model has helped bring about a sea change in the lives of millions, but the innovation there is not in technology: it is in the very business model. And one thing that the pre-paid mobile is not is cheaper. A pre-paid customer is actually cheaper for the network provider to service – money in advance; no cost of billing and collection – yet pays no less.

One of the greatest innovations of our times is the Grameen Bank model of microfinance: another that has affected the lives of millions but is neither based on technology nor cheaper. Grameen Bank offered not low-interest loans but small loans. It mitigated the high risk of lending to those whom other banks considered un-lendable with an acute understanding of the people it chose to serve, working through self-help groups of women and enabling borrowers to take small, short-term loans which they could repay in small, frequent instalments.

It is not that the borrowers of Grameen Bank are unique to Bangladesh or to poor Asian or African countries. The poor in the West are fewer, but their needs are exactly the same. Western bankers did not invent the model because that is not how they think. Not only is exactly the same model working in the United States today, it is Grameen Bank that is running it. With three offices already in New York City and others elsewhere, it is now opening three in the Bay Area with investment from Wells Fargo.

The curious case of change

What makes innovation in India remarkable is that for years Indian industry, protected internationally by import restrictions and domestically by the license-permit raj, operated in cost-plus mode: you toted up your costs and added a margin to determine your price, and it was not uncommon for manufacturers to take two or three price hikes in a year. It is only in the last fifteen years or so that both price and quality have been benchmarked by the competition and manufacturers have had to manage costs. (Wheel was a rare exception because Unilever chose to take the battle into the enemy's camp instead of deluding themselves that the cheap-and-nasty end of the market was not for them.)

It is tempting to get carried away with the exaggerated notion that the world has turned upside down as *The Economist* says it has, speaking of a new management paradigm and hailing the "new masters of management". But the new masters of management are really the old masters of management, who taught us in Marketing 101 to start with the consumer; that marketing is about meeting needs, and a product is only a delivery system.

Plus ça change, plus c'est la même chose. (The more things change, the more they remain the same.)

5

"I'M TOO SEXY FOR MY SHOES"

Or, what's gone wrong with the Tata Nano

When the Tata Nano was unveiled, the Haves groaned.

The triumphant arrival in Jan 2008 of the much-awaited People's Car was hailed around the world, but Indian car owners were not amused. They blanched at the prospect of those cheap little buggies breeding like cockroaches, jamming already overcrowded roads, and wished Mr Tata had left the Great Unwashed to their own devices.

Soon after came the crisis in Singur, then building the plant at Sanand, with limited supplies coming out of temporary facilities, and

---

[1] First published in *Campaign India*, 3rd Dec 2010. An enlarged and updated version appears in my book *Making Marketing Music* (New Delhi: Bloomsbury, 2019), titled 'What Went Wrong with Tata Nano?'

finally in June 2010 production commenced at the new 250,000-a-year plant. At last, enough for everyone.

But the People sat on their hands. You don't need data to see that something is not quite as expected, but the data support what you think you see: Nano sales have been dropping steadily month by month, from 9,000 in July to 3,000 in October, even as the passenger car market in the country has been surging.

So what's the matter?

It's not the product. It's spacious (I'm 6ft 3" tall, and I drive it comfortably); the air-conditioning is quick and effective; at 60 kmph it drives effortlessly and sits safely on the road; it parks like a dream; sips fuel delicately; and all that for Rs 1.70 lakh. It is now my preferred car if I'm driving to dinner and have to park in a typically crowded South Delhi colony or at a restaurant.

It's certainly not the manufacturer: it's Tata, and all that they represent.

Nor is it want of availability: I got mine in four days. That's great, but it also means, in a burgeoning car market, that not enough people want it. You may blame low supply for the low on-the-road numbers; but if a product is available off the shelf despite the low supply, clearly there isn't enough demand.

The problem of the Nano is it's cool: way too cool.

It's a symbol of contemporary India: not just standing toe-to-toe with the world but teaching it a thing or two. It's not cheap and nasty, it's cheap and cheerful and a product not of *jugaad* but of technological innovation. The Economic Times reports that the 67,000 Nano owners today include "corporate chieftains who otherwise ride on cars whose four wheels alone could buy the people's car". (Yours truly counts among the rest.)

Marketing people would give their eyeteeth to get their brand such a cachet. But the Nano has become the rich man's toy, to be bought on a whim, instead of a real car for real, hard-working middle-class families taking out a loan to get one. It doesn't even look like a real car – funny shape, no bonnet, and no boot. In a market accustomed to hatchbacks, it doesn't even have a hatch.

The problem of the Nano, though, is not what it is or how it looks, but that Tata Motors did not control the communication. To the extent that they did, they got caught up in the contemporariness of the Nano. Much of what they did was terrific for an upmarket, contemporary audience but bypassed the core.

The press reportage was so overwhelming and so positive that it was perhaps tempting to think it was enough and more. But the press did what they should have done, which was to be excited about Mr Tata's vision and its realisation, the technological achievement, national pride (and of course the Singur fracas and its aftermath). They did not fire the aspiration of the family on the scooter that inspired the vision, and assure them that this technological marvel was safe, reliable economical transportation, nor was it their job to. That was the job of the marketer.

It's not too late, since supply is still low. But when the cars start rolling out in large numbers and they do get around to managing the brand's communication, Tata Motors will have to focus on those for whom the Nano was intended, and risk forsaking those who have adopted it. Or that family will be riding a scooter a long time.

Nano went on to have a brief but chequered history. When sales were not responding the product went through several upgrades, and its advertising began to target young, hip first-time car buyers, but to no avail. There was some talk of an electric version to be made for Ola taxis. Sales dropped to 1,851 units in the financial year 2017–18. In June 2018 the company sold just three units, and made only one, and Tata Motors finally announced that was the end of the road for the Nano. A sad story, of a failure of marketing turning a brilliant product from a dream to the dust of reality in ten years.

6
A SERVICE IS NOT A PRODUCT

After weeks of resistance I succumbed to the iPad. The argument against was that there aren't many Wi-Fi hotspots in India, which limits your ability to use one. The answer was to get the one with 3G. That's not central to this story; it is only to say why I was in the market for a mobile phone connection.

Well, Saturday was Christmas and I was going to be travelling from the Monday, and you know how it is with tech toys: I wasn't going to wait until I returned and went to my office. And so it came to pass that on the Sunday after Christmas I was shopping for a mobile connection.

I chose Airtel – unsurprisingly, perhaps, given the 3G options available and the recent salience of the brand.

---

[1] First published as a blog post in January 2011. Enlarged and updated in my book *Making Marketing Music* (New Delhi: Bloomsbury, 2019).

From the website I got a list of outlets within a short radius of my home. It gave addresses and had columns for parking ('Yes' for all); timing (10 am to 8 pm for all); and the weekly day off (blank for all); but, strangely for a telecoms company, no telephone numbers.

I have Airtel landlines and ADSL at home and some kind of preferred customer status, so I called the designated customer service number. After wading through the IVR menu and getting a live human voice at the other end (Why do call centres speak to you in Hindi after you press 1 for English?) I was told this number was only for landlines and that I should call 98101 98101.

So I did. Asked where I should go for a new connection, the gent said, "You can get it where you buy recharge coupons."

"Ah, but I don't buy recharge coupons," I replied. "I need to get a mobile connection first."

"I'm trying to help you," he said. "If you don't find that helpful there's not much I can do," and hung up. Being well trained, though, he didn't forget to first say, "Thank you for calling Airtel."

I stubbornly called again and got someone else. She said that number was only for prepaid connections: for 'postpaid', as the term goes, I should call 98100 12345.

So I did. More IVR, about bill payment and value added services and so forth, and "to go back to the main menu press 1", or whatever. Oh, I missed what I needed. Back to the main menu. But I was right the first time: every conceivable kind of information was available except if you wanted a new connection.

Clearly, Airtel don't expect that if you want a new telephone connection you might use a telephone to help get one.

I got that list from the website and set out.

The first outlet was closed. And the second. And the third… "*Aaj* Sunday *hai na, ji*. (It's Sunday, you see)" If the website hadn't left the thoughtful 'weekly off' column thoughtlessly blank, or had given a phone number to call, I would have saved time and trouble. (It was right about parking, though, when it said 'Yes': there was a street outside each outlet.)

Four phone calls and an outing later I was no closer to a mobile connection.

Here is a company at the top of the heap; grown in hardly 20 years from small beginnings to a name to reckon with internationally; grown from selling cheap Chinese telephone instruments to mobile telephony to fixed telephony, broadband Internet and DTH. A single brand, a single website -- but not a single phone number.

Why would someone doing business in the 21st century and listing outlets not give their phone numbers?

What does it take for a telecoms company to think of having a universal toll-free phone number that anyone wishing to buy its services can call, to be directed by an IVR system to what they are looking for?

Mass-market services are often equated with fmcg, and services referred to as products. Years ago that not only sounded sexy, but also brought attention to the idea that a service had to be taken out to the user, not wait for the user to come to it, as had largely been the case in India. Now it only distracts attention from the fact that there is more to mass-market services than making them available "within an arm's reach of desire".

For fmcg the store is first a stocking point, its overriding role is convenience of access, and anyone going to any store gets the standardised product. The task of marketing is essentially to make the product available and attractive, and the brand experience lies in ownership and usage. Mass market services, on the other hand, are largely invisible and undifferentiated in use: it is in the interaction -- at the store, or on the telephone, or the Internet -- that the brand is delivered, by the sales assistant at the counter;

the call centre operator; or the guy who does all the boring detail on the website.

Marketers of products experience what they and their competitors sell, but marketers of services typically don't. Unless you call Customer Service or transact on the Internet or at the counter, you will never know how your customer receives your brand.

The quality of products from cars to candy is increasingly, over the last several years, benchmarked globally; but that of mass-market services is still benchmarked locally. It's a circular relationship: customers' expectations of services are limited by what they experience (shaped largely perhaps by the standards of the largest service provider, the government); and the services they get only cater to their low expectations.

It is ironical that even as the size of the services sector has surged to over 50% of the country's GDP, its quality remains mired in the bad old days.

7

MARKETING IS ABOUT PEOPLE

At a time when the marketing function is under siege, and the relevance of the CMO is in question, Nitin Paranjpe's call to marketers is even more relevant than when he made it in 2011.

At the recent World Marketing Congress in New Delhi Nitin Paranjpe, CEO of Hindustan Unilever[2], spoke eloquently for fmcg marketing professionals and, in the process, revisited what marketing is all about.

He observed that fmcg marketers are often apologetic or defensive about what they do for a living. In 21st-century India, where the challenges lie in technology, telecoms, infrastructure and financial services, it seems frivolous, almost embarrassing, he said, for grown-ups to be

---

[1] First published in *www.campaignindia.in*, Mar 2011, titled, "Marketing shampoo or Nano, you're changing lives".
[2] Now global COO at Unilever

engaged in peddling toothpaste, shampoo and the like.

But marketing affects people's lives. You and I take toothpaste and toilet soap, shampoo and detergent, for granted; but to many millions it is not just a better way to clean their teeth or hair; it is a move up in life. He spoke of a poor woman who uses a bit of moisturising lotion on dry skin and, with the feel and fragrance of it, feels beautiful for that brief moment. Think, he said feelingly, of the difference to her self-esteem: that is what you are doing for her.

Nitin's eloquent testimony brought back to mind a long-ago afternoon in a village in Kanyakumari district. I was standing at the back of a small crowd, to observe a rural van operation we were running to promote Pond's shampoo. (Yes, there was a Pond's shampoo, before Unilever acquired that company and the brand was focused on skincare.)

Our presenter was waxing eloquent and, as was his routine, called a small boy up, washed his hair, and sent him around the crowd so they could touch his hair and smell the fragrance of the shampoo.

A man standing next to me – not so young, unwashed, a daily wage farm labourer on a working day, by the look of him – went up to the front and bought one sachet of shampoo. As he returned, a man he was with wondered what he'd done that for. "It's for my wife," he said.

"You paid one rupee for that?"

"I don't think twice about paying a rupee for toddy. Why not to make her happy?"

A spontaneous gesture of spousal affection in a milieu you would least expect it in; later that afternoon, one happy woman feeling cared for; and, perhaps the following day, indulging in the experience as she bathed, and feeling sexy. What magic in a 5 ml sachet of something to which you and I give as much attention as we do to the air we breathe.

Years later we were working on Jai soap, a brand Hindustan Lever acquired when they bought Tata Oil Mills. To gain a close and deep understanding of the brand the Account Director on the business travelled to Jai's strong markets and called on a number of its users in their homes.

The key attribute of Jai soap was its jasmine fragrance. To us it was, even if you liked it, excessive. It obviously wasn't to its users but not, as you might derisively think, because they in their unsophisticated way liked that sort of thing. What came through in intimate womanly chats with users over cups of *chai* in their homes was its significance.

The fragrance of jasmine has both religious and sensuous connotations. In the life of a hard-pressed middle-class wife and mother, there is only one time in the whole day when she can be alone with herself and her dreams – when she bathes. The fragrance of Jai was not just a pleasant smell as she bathed, as lavender or musk may be to you; it fuelled a quiet romantic fantasy as she wallowed in the jasmine lather.

So powerful was the attraction of the fragrance that many a woman even kept the opened soap wrapper in her cupboard or trunk among her clothes. It was just a bar of soap; but it was a bar of soap that helped her feel special.

The same thought – the importance of bath time, or the potential of it – was behind the creation of Liril soap in the mid 70's. The girl in the waterfall represented exuberant freshness, but equally she represented exuberant sexuality. In a pre-television era when the monthly visit to the cinema gave the only audio-visual exposure most people had, she burned herself on the prospect's mental retina; and the unique green marbled soap and its lemon fragrance help trigger the feeling at bath time.

That all of these stories are about toiletries and sensuality is not to say that is the only way marketing affects, or can affect, people's lives! A prime example of its failure to do so is that of the Tata Nano.

The Nano is, famously, the result of Ratan Tata's vision for the ubiquitous family on the scooter and his mission of providing them safe, economical all-weather transport. The media celebrated the technological triumph and national pride, and the elite adopted the car as their plaything. No one told that family it was for them, and monthly sales plummeted to the low thousands.

Now there is an ad, but it's not from Tata Motors: it is from a bank offering auto loans for the Nano. The protagonist is a bus driver – not exactly an aspirational icon for the broad middle class. And as any student of marketing knows, upgrading to a car is aspiration first, functionality only second. I wonder if Tata Motors had anything to do with it. They've done the Nano a huge disservice either way[3].

Until about 15 years ago marketing in India was mostly about upgrading people from commodities to packaged goods and to newer product forms, and perhaps accompanying that was a sense of nobility of purpose. In the last few years branded competition has set in, and the volume of advertising has reached cacophonic levels. As we rush around frantically promoting discount offers and doing media deals with one eye on Cannes, Nitin's was a welcome reminder to all of us in the marketing value chain that there is more purpose to our work than we credit it with.

---

[3] For more on Tata Nano see p. 22, *"I'm too sexy for my shoes."*

8

LEADERSHIP, THE OLD-FASHIONED WAY

> *"Our plan is to lead the public with new products rather than ask them what they want. The public does not know what is possible, we do."*
>
> *-- Akio Morita, former Chairman, Sony Corp.*

The launch of the iPad2 has once again shifted the goalpost in the tablets game now being played with increasing intensity.

After selling 15 million iPads in nine months, Apple did again what they do best: change the level of the game. iPad 2 is a product no one asked for, a better version of a madly successful product that no one had asked for in the first

---

[1] First published in *www.campaignindia.in*, Apr 2011, titled, 'What really make the iPad cool'.

place. "There's nothing you will want more and need less," said early reviews.

We live, we are told, in a world of parity products, in which everything is the same, the differences only cosmetic. With competitive pricing and parity distribution, all that's left to do is to make an ad that you hope will break the clutter (and your agency hopes will win at Cannes) and throw lots of media money behind it. Yet here is a brand that has been built on terminally cool products. Apple was not the first to make anything: they just made everything better and – critically – different, based on the principle that "the best tools are those that users are not even aware they are using".

The iPod was not just the coolest device; it was the front end of a system that included iTunes. If having an iPod meant paying for downloading music, people were willing to do that too. If digital music has grown from nothing in 2001 (when iPod was launched) to a $26 billion category today, Apple has a lot to do with that.

Nor is the iPhone just a phone: it's the front end of a whole ecosystem and, truth to tell, every other smartphone today is just a substitute for it. Here's how desirable it is: according to one report, 50% of all thefts on the Paris metro are of smartphones, and 50% of those are of iPhone 3 and 4!

That's very well, I hear someone saying, but Apple makes technology products: surely you can't apply the same principle to everyday consumer products.

Consider Gillette, market leader for practically ever. While market leaders in many categories see shares shrink in the face of increasing competition though they remain leaders, Gillette even today has 70% of the global market for men's shaving blades and razors. Its continued dominance has been driven not by advertising, and least of all by pricing.

Driven by its unofficial motto, "There is a better way to shave, and we will find it," Gillette has repeatedly introduced better products to already-satisfied consumers. I've been through the whole gamut myself: starting as a teenager with 7 o'clock blades and a 2-piece razor, to the adjustable razor, to twin blade shaving systems from Trac II to Sensor to Contour, to Mach 3 in its successive upgrades. Every time Gillette introduces a new, better product millions of men faithfully drop what they are using and adopt the new one. The funny thing is that each time they not only switch to a product they didn't need, they also switch happily, in the process, to a more expensive one.

Of course you can't just make a better blade than Mach 3 and expect to beat Gillette at its own game: Gillette has built an unassailable position by continuously raising the barrier to entry. Nor, for that matter, can you make a cooler phone or tablet than Apple does. Better, maybe, but not cooler: because Apple defines cool, having built an unassailable position by being consistently at the cutting edge of both functionality and design.

That doesn't mean, though, that you can't lead with your product even today. Too many brands rely on advertising to make the difference for them. But Micromax challenged global brands slugging it out in the highly competitive Indian mobile handset market, on pricing – their most uncompetitive dimension – and shook up the market to become no. 2 to a much-diminished Nokia. Its full-featured handsets at never-before prices are supported with aggressive advertising, big media spends and big-ticket sponsorships, but the price is the differentiator. Its success has spawned me-toos, and it's too early to say what the future holds for Micromax, but the model is certainly sustainable.

What applies to products applies equally to services, and this is a good time to cite NTT Docomo. The market leader in Japan, it had a 50% share when mobile number portability was introduced. With 90% penetration the market was already saturated, and NTT Docomo had everything to lose. They shifted their focus entirely from acquisition to retention, fundamentally revamping all aspects of service to give customers no reason to want to switch – and successfully held share. With mobile number portability coming into India, all operators are in acquisition mode: which is fine, since none of them is dominant in any circle, but all of them seem to have taken retention for granted.

No doubt it is not enough to "build a better mousetrap"; it has to be marketed effectively. While Micromax outsources the product and focuses on marketing, Tata Motors developed and built the Nano ground-up to hit a price target and took marketing for granted. The results of both speak for themselves.

If there is a lesson in all this, it is that even today clear leadership is built the old-fashioned way: by delivering real value to customers, based on sustainable competitive advantage. That means delivering better products or services as well as connecting effectively with your customers.

9

IT'S NOT ABOUT THE ELEPHANT

> *It was six men of Indostan*
> *To learning much inclined*
> *Who went to see the Elephant*
> *(Though all of them were blind)*[2]

The problem with integrated marketing communications is that it has a name. It's no longer a concept or a way of thinking; it's a term. IMC, for short; or 360, as in, "We should do IMC," or, "We want a 360 plan."

Once upon a time it was just something you did; now we have a term for what we used to do, and instead of practicing it we lament that we are not, and have seminars about its whys and wherefores.

As a young Account Director I advised a client to use PR. When they said they didn't have the budget, I suggested they cut a few spots off the TV schedule and use that money to pay a PR firm,

---

[1] First published in *www.campaignindia.in*, April 2011
[2] John Godfrey Saxe, *The Blind Men and the Elephant*

which they did. It happened across the table: no presentation, no big deal. I did that because I thought it would help if the advertising were flanked by positive third-party communication. No one told me that was something called IMC.

When Philips launched epilators, we knew that no woman who wasn't familiar with the product would buy one without trying it. But how could she try one in a shop? So the ads offered a free in-home demo. A demo cost three times as much as the product, but the customer invariably invited others over, so each demo reached several women and a nice girlie time was had by all, and the demos seeded the product in a virgin market. Of course we also had in-shop product detailing and got the product featured in appropriate magazine columns. We did this because we thought our job was to get the product in the woman's hand, not just to run ads. No one told us this was 360-degree communication.

Cadbury wanted to run a campaign targeted at farmers in Kerala, to get more of them to plant cocoa. We ran advertising telling farmers why growing cocoa was profitable: but how was the farmer to know how to tend cocoa? Cadbury gave away subsidised seedlings; their experts visited farmers to advise them; newspapers published a series of articles on cocoa cultivation; All India Radio ran episodes on cocoa on their farm radio programmes; a network of cocoa collection centres was set up, an address list widely distributed, direction signs put up to point the way... The entire programme was conceived, devised and driven by the agency. We did that because we empathised with the farmer: all the client had asked for was advertising.

To promote the use of oral rehydration salts (ORS) in the treatment of diarrhoea in babies, we had to not only tell young mothers it was the right thing to do, we had to persuade doctors to prescribe ORS, and chemists to suggest it when asked for advice. We had to reach not only registered medical practitioners but, very critically, thousands of those not formally qualified, who are consulted by many an Indian family.

Time was when we were in the business of inducing consumers to do something. Now we are in the business of making ads, or buying media, or putting out mailers, or wearing whichever hat life has placed on our heads. It is no one's job but the marketer's to focus on the end result. We know IMC – or 360, take your pick – is a good thing, so we talk about it and regret that we don't do what we know we should.

So what's the problem with the term? It's not the specific term; it's the descent into jargon, which often gives the illusion of thinking. We used to think of the consumer. For Philips we asked how we could make it possible for her to try a product which is used in privacy; for Cadbury we asked how we could help the farmer get the necessary knowledge and guidance; and so on, and did what it took. Now we say we must do IMC, or 360, and ask what we should do in social media, and so on, so we can tick off each box.

The good news is that we in India aren't the only ones: it's the same globally. The bad news is that we in India aren't the only ones: it's the same globally. Just how mindlessly so came home to me when I saw a recent interview with Trevor Beattie on NDTV Profit.

Asked about integrated marketing communications, Beattie said it wasn't about just ticking boxes. So far, so good. He said what mattered was the quality of each thing you did. Oh, so now we know. If you do everything well, that's integrated marketing communications. But wait, there's more to it. He said it's the tone of voice that matters. And to illustrate he gave the example of his agency's work for FCUK in which, he said, the TV commercial, the posters, the store displays, and whatever else had exactly the same tone of voice. So what we learn from him is that you must tick all the boxes with the same colour of ink.

It's not that anything Beattie said was wrong; it's that he misses the point. Typically, he's thinking of what we do; he's not thinking of what we want the consumer to do, what comes in the way of their doing it, and what we need to do about that.

Trouble is, it's not about the elephant. We are the *mahout*, and it's about where we want the elephant to go. We think of the tools, and try to use as many of them as we can; we need to think instead about what we want to build, and use the tools needed to build it.

> *And so these men of Indostan*
> *Disputed loud and long.*
> *Each in his own opinion*
> *Exceeding stiff and strong,*
> *Though each was partly in the right,*
> *And all were in the wrong.*[3]

---

[3] Ibid.

10

"YOU'VE COME A LONG WAY, BABY!"[2]

How good were the good old days in Advertising, really?

Everywhere it's a picture of gloom and doom. I speak not of the crash of '09 and the now-you-see-it-now-you-don't recovery, but of the general mood in the advertising industry around the world.

From the annual 4A's conference in Texas in March to the annual AAAI conclave in Goa in April, the burden of the song was the same: revenue under pressure, scarcity of talent, rising talent costs, and no money to develop the talent pool.

As I sat at the Goa conclave I wondered how many of us, lamenting the state of affairs, have seen better days. How good were the good old

---

[1] First published in *campaignindia.co.in*, May 2011
[2] Advertisement for Virginia Slims cigarettes, 1968

days, really? To look beyond the rose-tinted rear view mirror I dug into my archives and found some data.

Let's get the overall perspective first. Total media expenditure in 2010 was Rs 29,411 crore. In 1985 it was Rs 449 crore. That's a compound annual growth rate of 18.25% for 25 years straight. Factor in long-term inflation and that's still way beyond GDP growth.

Back then advertising agencies earned 15% commission and handled pretty much everything, including printing, packaging design, and sales conferences, and made a hefty margin on artwork: so much so that if an agency's gross income was anything less than 17% of billing they had some serious questions to ask themselves.

No other compensation model was known, and clients largely paid on time, not the least because print was dominant (74% in 1985) and INS wielded a big stick. The closure of MCM, the original creative hotshop, and Aiyar's in 1975 due to defaulting on INS payments put paid to any stray thoughts anyone may have had on the subject.

Today there is no standard media commission, everything non-media is handled by someone else, and the standard for gross earning, made up of commission and fees, is probably more like 10% of billing.

In 1985-86 HTA (JWT), the largest agency in the country – which it has been since 1929, except when Alyque said it wasn't – had a gross billing of Rs 43.4 crore. On revenue of Rs 5.30 crore it made a profit before tax of Rs 36.5 lakh, or 6.8% of revenue, and after tax of Rs 2.8 lakh (0.5%). After paying Rs 2.5 lakh in dividend (it was a 100% employee-owned company) retained profit was Rs 30,000[3].

So the scale was small, but then the cost of everything was. (In 1974 the entire advertising industry billed Rs 95 crore, and the Times of India Bombay cost Rs 40 per col cm – equal to Rs 8 per sq cm). The lament – and the implication – is that if agencies today earned 15% commission like they used to they would be able to spend on all the things they should spend on, mainly talent and knowledge, as – by implication – they could then. Well...

In the late 70's the most profitable agencies, like OBM (O&M) and Everest, earned pre-tax profits of 15-25% of revenue. Global networks made 12-15% of revenue, but the norm in India was in the region of 6-8% (or, as a thumb rule, 1% of gross billing). Anything over that was

---

[3] The Economic Times, 9th Oct 1986

enviable. That's a far cry from today's norm of 20% of revenue.

Staff cost took the largest share of the revenue as it does today, except that then it typically took 65%. That was not because people were highly paid, but because there were so many of them. In those technology-less days dozens of artists painstakingly made physical artwork; armies of clerks in Media typed schedules, estimates and release orders on manual typewriters, hand-wrote registers, and managed thousands of film prints being exhibited in stand-alone cinemas all over the country; and other armies of clerks manned the Checking & Billing and Accounts departments.

Today we work in smart offices. 3,000 youngsters go to Goafest each year to celebrate their work and get to see and hear national and global big names. More and more people go to Cannes each year and do the same thing on an international scale. There's huge international exposure even in domestic agencies, because access is possible.

All of that was unthinkable then. After salaries and rent there was little left to do anything with. All we had was on-the-job training. Your bosses took you under their wing, took responsibility for you and taught you. Stern parents, they worked you to the bone, kicked your butt for your errors, and took quiet pride in your successes. We were underpaid and overworked, but we loved it.

The difference, you could say, is the difference in parenting. Mother's cooking has been replaced by branded foods in shiny packages, purportedly delicious *and* good for you; parental supervision, by paid professional care. Parents busy making it in the world have little time for their children. They buy them all that's desirable and send them to learn judo and ballet and tennis and pottery, and lament that the relationship isn't what they wish it were.

If we've gone from 17% revenue to 10%, that's because we undercut each other and devalue or worth. But we've also gone from 7% margin to 20%, with relatively fewer mouths to feed. We've come a long way: middle-class families who've made good.

As we enjoy our success we want our kids to have all that we didn't. But in the process we deprive them of the one thing we did have: care. If instead of rushing headlong all the time we paused for a moment and gave them quality time, then perhaps they would feel about us as we wish they did. Else we shouldn't be surprised if they fly the nest as soon as they grow wings.

11

THE STATE OF MARKETING IS WORRYING

The CMO Council has just released its 2011 State of Marketing Report. The outcome of a survey among 600 senior marketing professionals, mostly from North America and Western Europe, it throws up a disturbing picture of a professional community that finds itself unequal to the task at hand.

"We've found chief marketers overwhelmed with the day-to-day demands associated with strategic planning, branding, meeting, campaigning, and peer-level politicking," says the report. As a generalised statement that's pretty strong. What most of the survey participants are challenged by, or are struggling to deal with, boils down to technology and its outcomes: managing technology; managing data; and managing social media.

---

[1] First published in *campaignindia.co.in*, July 2011

What is at the top of the "to do" list of marketers in 2011?

- Multiplying marketing performance: to drive top-line growth and market share while better defining the brand and value proposition.
- Redefining customer experience
- Using insight to grow brand affinity

'Driving top-line growth and market share by better defining the brand and value proposition' neatly expresses the very role and purpose of the Marketing function, and is no different from what it has ever been. And 'using insight to grow brand affinity' is surely not new either: it is really *using insight* to *better define the brand and value proposition* to *drive top-line growth and market share.*

The trouble starts with what is meant here by 'redefining customer experience': essentially, customer experience on the web. It is almost as if customer experience is only virtual, or at least that it is all that matters. Much of the concern stems from the huge amount of unstructured data the digital media generate, which seems to demand to be used. The inability to access and integrate siloed data and make sense of what is accessible, on the one hand; and on the other, internal competition over data sovereignty and ineffective collaboration with IT groups, which have their own agenda, are frustrating chief marketers.

Marketers feel a strong need to "bridge the gap between the art of marketing and the science of analytics, measurement and process": they say they lack the competence to extract insights and predictive analytics from the mass of customer data that continues to multiply inside and outside their organisation.

Add to that the looming overhang of Social Media. Everyone knows it is something they ought to do – no chief marketer can go into a Board meeting with that box un-ticked – but most don't know quite what it is they should do. It is not unusual for a Social Media brief to be as vague as, "We want a Facebook page"; or to be as precise but meaningless as, "Objective: 1 million 'likes'." And then there are those who dismiss Social Media as being for kids. They aren't on Facebook; their kids are, so Social Media are not for grown-ups.

But it is not data and technology alone. "We've found chief marketers typically overwhelmed with the day-to-day demands associated with strategic planning, branding, meeting, campaigning, and peer-level politicking," says the CMO Council. In other words, with managing their lives.

It does seem strange that a whole functional area of management should feel so out of its depth. Consider, though, that in a rapidly changing world no function has to deal with change as much as Marketing does: mainly in society and technology, with all the implications they have for how people live; what moves them; what they buy and why; the choices available to them; and the ways to reach them.

In the United States today, for example, married couples with children are just 20% of all households. "From a marketing perspective this trend means that 'married with children' has become just another niche market," points out *Advertising Age*. "U.S. households are now so fragmented that any marketing effort to households must take into account that there are many more households of married with no children under age 18 (28%) or people who live alone (27%) than the 20% of households that are married with children." The happy family at the dining table is no more; the family in front of the TV is no more; media multitasking is the norm. The consumer is still not a moron, but she is not necessarily your wife anymore; and as likely as not, she is a he.

That is a transformational change that only Marketing, among all functions, has to deal with, and demands redefinition of the brand and value proposition and re-examination of its delivery. In this fast-changing, increasingly complex, multi-polar, multi-channel world, the Marketer must deal simultaneously with the strategic big picture and the minutiae of execution; make the creative leap as well as a hard-nosed justification of hard-won marketing budgets; and finally be answerable for top-line growth and brand profitability.

Small wonder that, as the report says, "Marketers are "distracted by greater pressure, complexities, and tactical execution challenges in the go-to-market process.... And they face pressure to better map and model the marketing mix, as well as substantiate and validate marketing spend."

That Marketing is overwhelmed is understandable. But why is it that among all the functions of management Marketing is the one most reluctant to turn to external expertise? Finance, Legal, Technology, Logistics, HR, you-name-it, call in consultants to help address specific issues or even to repurpose the entire function, or indeed the whole organisation. That makes sense. At the very least, it lets the managers get on with the business of running the business while someone outside the operating system deals with what is important but not immediate. It does much more, though. It brings to the task domain expertise and an informed but objective view.

Yet Marketing doesn't hire experts; it hires vendors. Historically, Marketing management for some reason expects, or is expected, to always know exactly what needs to be done. All it needs is someone to carry out its instructions. All manner of agencies – Market Research, Advertising, Media, CRM, PR, *et al* – present their views, but are paid not for their expert opinion but for execution.

This is perhaps because there is nothing technical about Marketing. It is at heart a creative, entrepreneurial function. Every day is a new day; every situation, unique. There is no template for success, and past experience is at best a rough guide. Market research and data analytics are valuable, but they can only help you make better-informed judgements: they can't mark out a guaranteed path to success. After all is said and done, the past studied and the data digested, it comes down to intuition and judgement.

If Marketing is uniquely complex, it is also uniquely resourced. More than any other function, Marketing has external expertise at its disposal. Executives at all levels routinely interact with specialists in Market Research, Media, Advertising, Design, *et al*, whose job it is to understand consumers in their various aspects. If I were battling my way in an increasingly complex, competitive, high-stakes world, I would listen carefully to them.

12

WANTED: MORE MAGIC, LESS LOGIC

> *"The brand manager – frequently a young marketing person on the way up the commercial ladder – sometimes uses temporary occupation of the brand to demonstrate flair and originality at the expense of brand consistency."*
>
> -- Wally Olins, in *Corporate Identity*

One day last week a small news item in *The Economic Times* caught my eye. "Dettol vs. Lux?" it asked, and reported that Reckitt Benckiser was extending Dettol into body wash. "After sparring with HUL's Lifebuoy in the anti-germ category for years," it said, "Reckitt is set to take on HUL's Lux in body washes." The line extension into body wash seemed natural. The bit about Lux didn't.

Over 75 years old in India, Dettol is a defining brand. 'Clean and safe' has a smell: the smell of Dettol. The smell of a hospital is the smell of

---

[1] First published in *www.campaignindia.in*, Nov 2011

Dettol. A bottle sits on many a bathroom shelf, often unused for months or even years but giving the quiet reassurance that it is there and you don't have to worry about nasty germs. "Dettol protects" was its simple, confident tagline for many years.

Of course there is a limit to which domestic use of liquid antiseptic can and will grow. But if you owned a brand as powerful as Dettol you wouldn't shrug your shoulders and say, "I guess that's about it": you would want to leverage its equity to look for new ways of meeting consumer needs – in other words, line extension. So far, so good; but the question is, line extension into what?

It was in the late 1980's, if I'm not mistaken, that Reckitt first forayed in that direction, with Dettol Soap. The antiseptic property of Dettol was interpreted, with what often passes off for deeply insightful thinking, to lead to a so-called higher-order benefit – antiseptic, therefore protection, therefore care – and the soap was dubbed 'The Love and Care Soap'.

Of course that didn't work. Neither was Dettol about love and care, nor was the mother so wanting for expressions of love and care that she had to reach out to Dettol for one. Repositioned later to offer a "100% bath" – as a result of its antiseptic property – Dettol soap grew to be a very strong player in premium toilet soaps.

The soap became the primary form in which consumers interacted with Dettol, but it was the liquid antiseptic that gave meaning to Dettol soap.

The story is not in itself remarkable. What makes it so is that this was only the beginning of Reckitt's many failed attempts over the years to make Dettol what it is not. And it would seem from the reported intention to take on Lux that they haven't done with the idea.

Apart from the perfectly sensible hand-wash liquid Reckitt have, over the years, launched Dettol shaving cream, mouthwash, prickly heat powder, anti-dandruff shampoo and floor cleaner, among other products: most dead, some perhaps on life-support systems. And in toilet soaps, moisturising soap (Dettol Extra) and glycerine soap (Dettol Junior). The argument was that all of these products protect – against dryness, against dandruff, against prickly heat. "Dettol protects", remember?

The argument for Dettol moisturising soap was that research showed (The graveyard of marketing is full of products whose conception began with someone saying, "Research shows...") that many people didn't like Dettol soap because it smells of Dettol; and they didn't like the colour; and they didn't particularly feel the need for a germicidal soap. So Dettol moisturising soap was meant to enable you to use Dettol soap that didn't look or smell like Dettol or do what Dettol does. Why would you want to? Now Dettol body wash comes in four variants: Original, Skincare, Cool and Fresh, for possibly the same reason.

That's all very well, you may say, but what should Reckitt have done? Well, they didn't have far to look. Dettol in the UK has a wide range of product offerings, all of them anti-bacterial, in two broad sub-brands: Healthy Touch and Complete Clean. All have the predominantly green Dettol graphics: not a pink or a blue among them. I have no idea of their history or how much each of them contributes to the Dettol kitty, but as an observer I see an inarguable consistency in the brand proposition as well as the presentation.

Dettol is not alone, though. Consider Dove. Once upon a time I knew what Dove was: one-quarter moisturising cream, so it keeps your skin soft while it cleans. I could understand Dove body wash, and face wash. Now there is a range of Dove shampoos, to keep hair soft by keeping it damage-free; prevent hair fall; and protect your hair and strengthen it, among other wonderful things they do, because (I'm not making this up; you can see the ads) they are one-quarter moisturising milk. As if that was not enough, there is Dove deodorant, which nourishes your underarms and makes them fair in seven days because – you guessed it – it is one-quarter moisturising cream. Is there somewhere a Dove beauty bar or body wash that keeps your skin soft? I forget.

Then there is Garnier. Dove, to be fair, is based on a single product attribute, stretched though it may be, and there is an identifiable Dove look. Garnier has products for practically every part of the body, for both sexes, with little in common in terms of product attribute, tone and style, or brand vocabulary. If you look at a reel of Garnier commercials, it seems anything goes as long as at the end of the ad someone breathlessly says, "Take care."

The products are perhaps selling, in larger or smaller quantities. But just as strong brands take long to build, they take long to get damaged. Dettol, despite everything, continues to feature in the top ten in the Brand Equity list of India's most trusted brands.

It is not that you can't stretch a brand into seemingly unrelated products: there is perhaps no better example in the world than Apple, going from computers to music players to mobile phones, changing the game in each category and stamping it with the unmistakable Apple brand. To do that you need to have a very strong sense of what the brand is and can be to its consumers, and that is largely a creative leap, not the reasoned, numbers-driven, left-brain argument that Marketing has become.

It is good to see, in this milieu, one global leader declaring that it will bring back the magic, and reward marketers who are prepared to take risks and back creative ideas. Outlining a ten-year marketing perspective to their global brand teams recently, Unilever's top marketing executives emphasised the need to move away from "unthinking adherence to quantitative market research at the risk of losing some of the creative spark that leads to great creative ideas". Amen.

13

CROWDSOURCING: NO SAFETY IN NUMBERS

'Unilever to boost reliance on crowdsourcing with eYeka'
— *News item*

"[Lowe] have created a very strong creative vehicle that's extremely well defined and portable. But their work has created a problem for them, because it makes Peperami the obvious candidate for crowdsourcing." That's how a Unilever London spokesperson explained it when, two years ago, the company fired the advertising agency on Peperami, in favour of crowdsourcing.

Some compliment! Can you see the agency head calling in the Peperami team? "Folks, I've just returned from lunch with John Client. Peperami is tracking superbly on every parameter. You've created one of those rare great brand properties

---
[1] First published in *www.mxmindia.com*, June 2013

that will stay with the brand for many, many years. Unilever have paid you the ultimate compliment: we're fired. From now the public will make the ads.

"Jean, pop the bubbly. I'm proud of you guys. You are our A Team, and here's an A Team challenge for you. I am assigning you to our biggest Unilever brand: get fired on it within the year. A special Christmas bonus if you make it. Cheers, and more power to your elbow."

If the idea itself is strange, the outcome was bizarre. Unilever received 1,185 entries and selected not one but two submissions (Both of which came from laid-off advertising professionals: a copywriter from London and a former creative director from Germany. So much for the crowd.), and announced that they would combine the two ideas to make the new campaign. "We're certain the two ideas will be a successful campaign," said the Peperami marketing manager. That, from the company which taught us that every advertisement must be based on a "Single Selling Idea" – the first of the ten Unilever Principles of Great Advertising. Whether Unilever's winning Advertiser of the Year at Cannes that year was because of Peperami or despite it we don't know.

Meanwhile, Kraft Foods in Australia crowdsourced the name for the new cheese variant of its iconic bread spread Vegemite, and chose – hold your breath – iSnack 2.0. "The name Vegemite iSnack 2.0 was chosen based on its personal call to action, relevance to snacking (I snack, get it?), and clear identification of a new and different Vegemite (2.0, wow!) to the original," said a Kraft spokesperson. "We believe these three components completely encapsulate the new brand." Consumers didn't, apparently. Following a furore, Kraft rather tamely put out a list for people to choose from, and equally tamely changed the name to a blasé Vegemite Cheesybite.

Around the same time Frito-Lay in India sought ideas for new flavours of chips. To the credit of Frito-Lay it must be said that they weren't chintzy – on the contrary, they generously spent more than they might have had they done conventional market research instead. For four shortlisted flavours they awarded a prize of Rs 5 lakh each – a total of Rs 20 lakh or over US$ 40,000, way more than Unilever London paid to get a new idea for Peperami. The prize for the ultimate winner was Rs 50 lakh (over US$ 100,000) and 1 per cent of sales revenue.

Frito-Lay were truly generous, but all they did was essentially to solicit consumer opinion on a new product, which might otherwise have been done by conventional market research. Meanwhile other marketers like GE, General Mills, Pepsi, Dell and Starbucks have been seeking everything from product and service ideas to, reportedly, inputs on agency selection and media placement. Crowdsourcing shops have come up which will brief the crowd and filter the solutions, as Idea Bounty did for Peperami.

That's awfully interesting. Suppose one day Lowe had told Unilever, "You'll be delighted to know we've increased the creative strength on your business. We've fired your entire creative team. Now, instead of being limited to a handful of people under our roof, we'll put our briefs on your brands out on the Internet and get ideas from hundreds, if not thousands." Might they have saved the Peperami account? I don't know about you, but I can't see a delighted client congratulating the agency on its farsighted initiative.

Proponents of crowdsourcing cite the 'wisdom of crowds', propounded by Surowiecki in his book of the same name. "I don't think people realize how powerful the crowd can be when engaged on working on a good idea," says one. Perhaps, but this is not the crowd working on a good idea; it is a multitude of individuals independently developing ideas. They're not building on each other's thoughts; there's no cross-fertilization of thinking.

Diversity, independence and decentralization are three of the four "elements required to form a wise crowd" that Surowiecki lists: "Diversity and independence are important because the best collective decisions are the product of disagreement and contest, not consensus or compromise." But 1,185 responses to a brief from perhaps as many people working independently of each other do not constitute collective thinking, and are not the product of disagreement and contest.

Surowiecki's fourth element is aggregation: in this context, the marketing management of the company deciding – singly, collectively or sequentially – among the shortlisted submissions. So it is finally down to the quality of decision-making. If you decide on iSnack 2.0, it doesn't matter whether the submissions come from the crowd through a crowdsourcing agency, or from known people through an advertising agency.

That the advertising agency has designated, informed people and institutional memory is only one of its advantages over a crowd. The other is that if you make bad decisions you can always blame the agency and fire it. You can't fire a crowd.

14

MARKETING FORGOT HIM – AND THAT SHOWS

Jack Trout passed away on 5th June 2017. In remembrance, The Smart Manager *invited tributes to the man who coined the concept of Positioning. Here's mine.*

Whether the concept of Positioning is thriving or has gone the way of the USP and the dodo may be arguable, but Jack Trout's most important work was perhaps his 2006 book *In Search of the Obvious*, aptly subtitled 'The Antidote to Today's Marketing Mess'.

"While CMOs are being fired and US brands are descending into chaos, confusion and commoditisation," Trout writes, "US consultants are producing book after book about what should be done about the mess."

---

[1] First published in *The Smart Manager*, Jul-Aug 2017

That is exactly what he's done too, you may say. The difference, though, is that Trout argues against the arcane concepts, catchphrases and esoteric jargon that have become the stuff of marketing. "You can easily sum it all up by observing that marketing is increasingly becoming a complex science of data mining, number slicing, niche segmenting, and so on and on. As I said, marketing is a mess."

Taking inspiration from Robert Updegraff's *Obvious Adams,* Trout makes the case for common sense, which was really the unifying theme in everything he wrote and said. The trouble, as Updegraff wrote, is that the obvious seems simple and commonplace, but we like clever ideas and ingenious plans. And those who tell us to get our heads out of our computers, to think simply, and to speak and write simple English, make us uncomfortable and insecure.

Current marketing literature and the discussions on marketing forums show a profession in search of a role and meaning. The biggest concerns of CMOs seem to be digital and social media, and managing and making sense of data. But the Internet, and all that it spawns, "is not the ultimate solution," as Trout says. It is "only a new way to reach people with your obvious idea." And if that is what keeps CMOs up at night, rather than the pressures of driving top line growth by consistently delivering a competitive value proposition, it is small wonder that, as they lament, not more of them become CEOs.

Thankfully there are the few beacons, the iconic practitioners of the Obvious Adams philosophy. And there is no better exponent of it than Google. It's not just technology that keeps the brand where it is; it's what they do with it and – most important – why.

Google's stated mission is "to organize the world's information and make it universally accessible and useful", and everything they do is to serve that single purpose. Google neither was the first search engine nor is it the only one, yet it has a global market share of 78% in desktop access and 95% in mobile and tablet access. Ten years ago Yahoo's mission was to be no. 1 in mobile search. Now its market share is 1.7% and the company is in the ICU.

It is not a coincidence that Google is one of the two most valuable brands in the world (alongside Apple) on all the major brand valuation reports: those of Interbrand, Millward Brown (Brand Z) and Forbes.

With technology brands one may wonder how much proprietary technology contributes to their success, so consider a consumer brand: Gillette, which has dominated the market for men's shaving blades for over 100 years, and even today has over 70% of the global market.

Gillette is driven by its unofficial motto, "There is a better way to shave, and we will find it." It has repeatedly introduced better products to already-satisfied consumers, who faithfully drop what they are using and adopt the new, more expensive one. It has built an unassailable position by focusing on one thing and, by excelling at it, continuously raised the barrier to entry.

Result: In Interbrand's listing of the world's most valuable brands Gillette at no. 16 is the no. 1 Personal Care brand, and has been from the beginning.

Closer home and down the technology scale is Amul, aptly described in *Melt* as "the number one nobody talks about'. With a turnover of Rs 38,000 crore[2] the Amul brand is bigger than the total turnover of Hindustan Unilever (Rs 34,000 crore).

What keeps Amul there? In a word, trust. At a time when, as the Edelman Trust Barometer reports, consumers' trust in brands is declining as marketers cut corners and even blatantly deceive consumers, here is a brand built on trust – and uncomplicated thinking. And, in a low-technology business, they have kept the barrier to entry very high, delivering uncompromising quality at prices that are

---

[2] Cited by R S Sodhi, Managing Director, GCMMF, in *Melt*, June 2017

unviable for competition, by maximising marketing efficiencies.

The search for the obvious begins and ends, says Trout, with the Chief Executive Officer. With the pressures of the stock markets and of PE investors and the resulting focus on short-term results, CEOs need to show they are doing something. But the tougher, the more complex the environment, the more important it is to know what *not* to do, which road not to take. The trick is to know where you are going. If you don't know where you are going, any road will get you there.

MEDIA
AND
MEDIA REGULATION

15

AS YE SOW...

I wrote this piece in April 2010. Sadly, nothing has changed in the nine or ten years since – at least, not for the better.

'One of the most powerful men in global media' asked his audience to vote on where media agencies fit in the communications structure. When they voted strategic, he disagreed. Unless things changed drastically, he said, media agencies would be in the 'leverage or acquisition category'; media owners were more likely to be in the strategic category.

"Have media agencies equipped and evolved themselves like media owners have?" asked Kester Fielding, Director of Global Media Procurement at Diageo, speaking at the Festival of Media in Valencia yesterday. "How can media agencies better communicate to clients

---

[1] Blog post first published in Apr 2010

that they are working in their best interests?" Media agencies were still having the same conversations they did a decade back, he said, and it was about time that changed.

No, Mr Fielding, they are not: you are, and it's time that changed. Agencies are now engaged in the conversation you started. Back then media was a Marketing function and was called Media Management; now, apparently, it is a commercial function and is called Media Procurement.

It's bemusing that a leading advertiser should place media owners higher up the strategic value chain than media agencies. Advertisers don't hire a media house: they hire a media agency, to help get the best value for their media money. All media space and time is a commodity until you can see the differential value media vehicles represent in relation to the strategy of a particular brand at a particular time. Determining and getting that incremental value for the client and the brand is the agency's job. In fact, a truly sophisticated marketer will talk to their media agency before they brief their creative agency.

Time was when media agencies were in the business of advising their clients on the deployment of media budgets: not just how much to pay for media but where, how and how much to advertise. Buying was a backroom function, its job to buy the desired plan at the best possible price; now it is not only client-facing, it is almost the *raison d'etre* of the agency.

Time was when the advertising agency had a seat at the client's top table, because top management looked to it for strategic counsel. It reduced itself to an ad provider; and its seat was taken by the media agency, which had the perspective on where the market was and how best it could be reached. For many marketers their advertising budget is the single largest line item after the cost of raw material (for Diageo, reportedly, its largest, even more than glass bottles for its portfolio of alcohol brands), and the media agency influenced the deployment and direction of that money.

The media agency may still have that seat, but now sits on it wearing its buyer hat and tells cost-pressured clients how much money it has saved. The media planner has been relegated to providing an intellectual fig leaf to new business pitches; retrofitting plans to deals; and doing post-buy analyses to justify deals – and to making media scene presentations to visiting dignitaries.

The responsibility for this change must lie with the marketer. A media agency is a service provider and is bound to be oriented to what its clients seek. As long as it is judged primarily by price – how cheaply it buys media and how little it charges for its services – that is what it will focus on delivering. Why, after all, would you strive to deliver strategic value if that is not what you are hired, assessed and paid for?

Mr Fielding is only symptomatic of a larger malaise afflicting marketing. The bean counters have taken over – and that was long before Lehman Brothers collapsed. Creativity is only a word, and you don't take your right brain to work. The latest and most worrisome manifestation of that is the just-released report of the CMO Council[2].

"My challenge to [media agencies] is to communicate their value far better than they do," said Mr Fielding. My challenge to Mr Fielding is this: engage with your media agency often enough and well enough to know what effort they are making on your behalf; use cost efficiency measures to manage your budget but don't make them the be-all and end-all of your agency's job; pay your agency in fees, not in commission, and give it a bonus based on brand track scores; and if you don't trust your agency's professional integrity to be true to its job in this compensation regime, fire it.

---

[2]   See p. 1, The End of the World as We Know It?

16

"EVERYBODY HAS WON, AND ALL MUST HAVE PRIZES."[2]

For several years now analysts have predicted the end of television. The ubiquity of the Internet, and now of mobile telephony, enables people to watch what they want to, where they want to, when they want to, instead of having to be where the box is, at a time the broadcaster chooses to make available what they want to watch. Given the freedom to choose time and place, who would want to be tied down?

That is of course perfectly logical, but people don't always behave logically. Even as marketers and media analysts were discovering digital/online media and predicting the end of television, people were buying more TVs: Nielsen reports that US households owning 3 or more TVs grew from 41% ten years ago to 55% in 2010.

---

[1] First published in *The Smart Manager*, Sep-Oct 2010
[2] The Dodo in *Alice in Wonderland*

The last American TV upfront selling season gave doomsayers something to think about. Marketers and media buyers, who had long been questioning the effectiveness of TV, complaining about audience measurement, critical of the anticipated price increases and extolling the virtues of the Internet, voted with their cheque books, paying 7-10% higher prices to buy large portions of the 2010 inventory of the networks' top shows. Result: after a flat 2008 and a fall in 2009, US ad spend on TV is expected to grow in 2010.

Meanwhile, across the pond in the UK it is television that is slated to drive overall ad spend growth in 2010, following a decline last year.

Two-timing but faithful

Marketers and their cohorts have discovered afresh the merits of mass media, and media axioms have become the new media wisdom. The Chief Investment Officer at Group M, quoted in *Advertising Age*, had his epiphany when he realised that, "In online video, if you try to reach the audience you get on national television, it will cost you more [per customer]. You have to be able to put together a lot of inventory [to be able to reach that level of unique viewers]." An analyst at Ernst & Young[3] lauded TV's fundamental value of delivering a large-scale

---

[3] Now EY

audience efficiently: "You can't get it elsewhere. That's the difference between television and various types of online." (That's not the only difference, but more on that later.)

So is all the hoopla about the Internet just that: hoopla? What are people doing—watching TV or using the Internet?

The correct answer is, both. Studies in the last ten years have shown that increased demand on people's time is met with an increase in supply, by multitasking. Anyone who has a teenager at home has seen them talk on the phone, surf the net, watch TV and listen to music at the same time.

The teenager in your home is not alone: theirs is a multitasking generation. One study shows they engage in as many as 44 hours of activity in a day, performing on the average two to three other tasks while watching TV. A 2004 US study found 8-18 year olds were taking in eight-and-a-half hours of media consumption in six-and-a-half hours a day. When repeated in 2009, it found them taking in ten-and-a-half hours of consumption in seven-and-a-half hours a day. A study in Tokyo found in 2009 people spending 60 minutes a day at home on the Internet or a mobile phone, against four minutes in 2000; but they also spent 216 minutes in front of the TV, from 206 in 2000.

We don't have multitasking data for India, but IRS 2010 R2 tells us that from 7 to 9 pm, when 45% of the whole TV audience universe is watching TV, 72% of Internet users are doing so. In fact, in any given time band Internet users are more likely to be watching TV than non-users are.

So the share of TV in media consumption has gone down – as a dominant market leader inevitably loses share to new entrants – but its consumption in absolute terms has not.

Media multitasking is not limited to teenagers. Look around you: all of us are on the phone, sms or email as we watch TV. The difference is only of degree. Of course that means the TV doesn't have our fullest attention; but equally it means the Internet, or for that matter the newspaper, doesn't either.

Multitasking is why the consumption of TV doesn't go down even as that of other media goes up. But what keeps people in front the TV set when they don't have to be? Why, when they can watch on computers and mobile phones when and where they wish to, do they continue to watch on the conventional television set at home, as it is transmitted?

The bigger hammer...

Perhaps the least understood fact about TV is that watching it is a social activity. People want to watch what they want to, but even more they want to watch together. What matters is not whether you watch it on the TV set or on a computer or a mobile phone: what matters is that you watch it when others do, even if they are not in the same place. In a Facebook and Twitter world it is not necessary to be together to share: people connect and share with people who are not in the same physical space. In fact people routinely connect and share with people they don't otherwise know and have never met except in the virtual space.

That is why, as Newsweek reports, quoting Nielsen data, 99% of TV viewing in the US is live. Interestingly, even DVR viewing takes place substantially in the next hour after a live telecast, and web TV viewership peaks within one day of the original airing, which suggests that those who record a show or access it later on the Internet do so because they were busy watching something else live at the time.

The family clustered in front of the TV may have practically disappeared in the West, but it continues to be the norm in India. Of the 110 million Cable and Satellite TV (C&S) homes in the country, 97% have a single TV[4]. Even in the metros, single-TV homes are 86% of the TV-owning universe. The TV is typically on all evening, with the whole family typically sitting in front of it. (Given the preponderance of single- and two-room homes, there aren't too many other places to go.)

This is confirmed by TV viewership data: if family drama soap operas reach more men than any other kind of programming does, that is not because Indian men are peculiar but because they happen to be in the room at the time and get counted. Audience measurement research tells you who's in front of the TV; it cannot tell you how engaged they are.

Against 492 million C&S viewers in the country, there are 52 million regular (defined as at least once a month) Internet users, and eight million broadband connections. 20 million users claim to have a broadband connection at home, and 50% of them claim to watch video on the Internet, giving you a potential 10 million web video viewers.

Does that mean there is no place for the Internet in marketing? Of course there is.

---

[4] 2018 update: Of 197 million TV owning homes, 4 million have more than one TV, i.e., 98% are single-TV homes. (Source: EY report, *A billion screens of opportunity,* March 2019, citing the Broadcast India survey 2018.)

...and the sharper nail

First, a sense of scale: more of the affluent use the Internet than read English magazines or business dailies, so the number is nothing to be scoffed at. It looks small when you make the wrong comparison, with TV.

Second, if your audience is mostly male, relatively young and relatively affluent—or even if, out of a wider audience, that demographic is important to you—the Internet must be integral to your marketing program.

Too fragmented to get you a mass audience, the Internet enables you to target special interest groups: from definitions as broad as cricket or movie fans to dog lovers to as narrow as antique watch collectors, and all sorts in between.

You can also target people in context. A print ad or a TV commercial runs in a specific position or at a specific time, and treats all readers and viewers as equal. On the Internet, a bank, for instance, can deliver a home finance message to one person and an auto finance message to another, depending on what they are doing on the Internet at that time.

More, it is not a passive, lean-back medium like TV is: it enables active engagement. On the Internet people do things—seek information, examine products, answer questions, share with others, buy. On the TV, they typically just watch.

The trouble is the digital space is growing rapidly not only in size but in complexity, developing faster than most can keep pace with it, and abounds in jargon and buzzwords, making anyone but the most engaged feel at least mildly ignorant. It also throws up huge volumes of data, giving marketers the reassuring feeling that at least in that space they have the answer to their eternal question: which half of their money is being wasted.

Consequently, many marketers approach digital media from the fear of being left out, rather than from wanting to leverage an opportunity to engage with their audiences. What they do is in response to the question, "How should we use digital?" rather than, "How should we better engage with our customers?"

The Chief Marketing Officer of Unilever seemed to betray that kind of thinking when he said at Cannes this summer that the company will spend money on digital media in proportion to the time people spend on it: that in the US, where people spend 25% of their time on the Internet, Unilever would spend around 20% of its money on it. The company has doubled its US digital spending this year, but a huge amount of that has reportedly been on talent fees paid to baseball stars for an online-only campaign for Dove!

What matters is not how much money you spend but what you do: how much you spend is only a consequence of that.

Different strokes for different folks

The "broadband is the new broadcast" kind of thinking was thus far largely in the West, with its near-universal Internet penetration and widespread broadband access. Of late, however, the murmur is being heard in India too, especially amongst those targeting younger audiences.

Whether the Internet is more developed or less, it is not a question of either-or, as many would have us believe. And there is no reason why it should be, any more than for TV and newspapers or TV and radio.

The role of the media in advertising is to connect marketers with their audiences, and people lead multimedia lives. As people go about their lives they read newspapers and magazines, watch television, listen to the radio, access the Internet, and so on. You may choose to focus your resources on one, as a matter of strategy or of necessity, or use a combination. Which ones you choose and how you use them must depend on the task at hand. Rarely does it make sense to use all.

Media choice is always a trade-off against the large scale, high efficiency and control over content and scheduling that mass media advertising offers; the small volume but active engagement of the Internet; the small volume but sharp targeting of direct marketing; the high credibility but low control of PR; high engagement but small scale of event marketing; etc.

Different marketers, even those in seemingly similar circumstances, will make different decisions as to what to give up in favour of what, and there isn't one right answer. There is one wrong answer, though, and that is to do something only because you are afraid of not doing it.

17

ALL NEWS IS GOOD NEWS

First, the headlines:

- *CNN-IBN is the No. 1 English news channel*
- *News X is the No. 1 news channel*
- *News X is the No. 1 news channel in Bengaluru*
- *India's top 13 news shows across all English news channels are from CNN-IBN (Making it No. 1)*
- *CNN-IBN achieved absolute leadership* (i.e., was or became No. 1) *in the financial year*
- *CNN-IBN was India's most watched* (i.e., No. 1) *English news channel during the Ayodhya verdict week*
- *When the Ayodhya judgement was decided... Times NOW was the most trusted channel* (i.e., No. 1)
- *During the Ayodhya verdict, India shunned all other news and entertainment channels, to tune in to Aaj Tak.* (In other words, Aaj Tak was No. 1)

---

[1] First published in *agencyfaqs.com*, Nov 2010

- *Zee News is no. 1 in the top 8 metros*
- *IBN7 is no. 1 Hindi News Channel in the last 13 weeks*

These are not conflicting statements. But when you see the ads from which these claims are quoted, notice the asterisk: conditions apply. It seems that at every news channel there is someone whose job is to slice and dice TAM data until they find a combination of audience, markets, and dayparts in which that channel is No. 1.

The most prolific of these data analysts seems to work at CNN-IBN[2]. To claim its leadership during the Ayodhya week the channel defined eight different audience groups; for its claim of being the no. 1 English news channel, three; for absolute leadership in the financial year, four; and to claim all 13 top news shows, one. So as a marketer or a media planner for which audience am I supposed to think of CNN-IBN?

But CNN-IBN is by no means alone.

IBN7 is the No.1 Hindi news channel in the last 13 weeks – among 25-44 year olds; in Delhi; in some random 13 weeks that happen to suit IBN7.

News X makes an unqualified claim of being "The #1 News Channel" based on having the

---

[2] Now CNN News 18

highest share among English news channels in six metros on one particular Sunday.

Aaj Tak has turned to the IRS, and zoomed out its competitive frame from news channels to include GECs. IRS, for TV? Whom is that supposed to impress?

NDTV 24X7 has gone further: ignoring TV audience research altogether. Some years ago, finding TAM data didn't suit their purpose, they turned to aMap. Now that doesn't work for them either, so their latest ads cite "three [unnamed] major surveys across India" to claim 60% viewership among an undefined audience.

News channels indulge the most, among all broadcasters, in obfuscation and half-truths. That is the genre that you would think should value credibility. If I lied about myself all the time, would you trust me to tell the truth about everything else?

Even those who actually have a story don't tell it. And that includes NDTV 24X7. The brand still has strong equity, but instead of leveraging that and giving you a reason to watch the channel or to buy advertising on it, they have resorted to telling half-truths to claim numerical leadership that they lost long ago.

Times Now does have differentiated content, which has been the driving force behind its sustained leadership. Ironically, the difference is news. Over 80% of Times Now content is what TAM classifies as 'New Bulletins'; for NDTV 24X7 it is about 55%. But its tag line "Always with the news" is now only a tag line, while its ads are all about being no. 1. Times Now is at least clear and consistent in its audience definition: Male, 25+, SEC AB, 1mn+ markets.

And then there is Aaj Tak. With India TV and Star News breathing hotly down its neck, its leadership on a daily basis is more and more tenuous; but whenever there is a big news event viewers move en masse to Aaj Tak. What does Aaj Tak do with that? Nothing. Just keeps finding newer, and increasingly obscure, reasons to make the No.1 claim.

Everyone has the same data (except NDTV's unnamed 'major surveys'), and no buyer worth taking seriously goes by a broadcaster's analysis, much less by the way they use that data in an ad. Yet they continue to put it out.

Do news broadcasters as a class really have such a poor understanding of how their customers buy? Or is their advertising targeted at naive new advertisers? Or perhaps it is just an expensive in-joke, intended only to cock a snook at each other.

18

MIRROR, MIRROR, ON THE WALL…

Outlook celebrated its 15th anniversary by telling us comprehensively what is wrong with the media.

In the first half of its 314-page anniversary issue, 'Media in Crisis', journalists, critics and others lament the state of the media. (The notable exception, perhaps, is Ravi Dhariwal, stoutly articulating the *Times of India*'s oft-stated position on oft-raised issues.)

Self-flagellation is one thing; flogging the whole community is quite another. When you proclaim loudly what is wrong with everyone, you imply that such is not the case with you. And the second half of the issue celebrates 15 glorious years of the balanced, independent journalism of *Outlook*.

The first half is easy to read. It takes as long as it does to flip through its pages, because all you need to read is the title of each piece and the accompanying blurb; the rest is detail. In fact it

---

[1] Blog post first published in Nov 2010

takes even less. All you have to do is go through this sampling of titles and blurbs:

- *Media subdues the public. It's so in India, certainly* – Naom Chomsky
- *Why I quit the media: A mega sellout! Journalism outspaced (sic), it was time to put my pen down* – Sumir Lal
- *Cut-Rate Democracy: Pay and they will publish you. It's a short stop to doomsday from here for our media.* – Paranjoy Guha-Thakurta
- *Reading the Reader: There will always be a market for analysis. But will marketers see that in the inkblot?* – Patrick French
- *What the Hack!: The media would do well to heed political and world events than (sic) affaires d'amour* – Shashi Tharoor
- *Pow! Thud! Dis!: You heard it on this channel first. On every channel actually.* – Mark Tully
- *Mainland Discourse: The media ignores basic facts about the Northeast, J&K in its insurgency chatter* – Sanjoy Hazarika
- *Just Bite, Don't Chew: Reasoned, informed talk is out of place on the idiot box. TRPs set the agenda.* – Dipankar Gupta

You get the idea.

The section begins with a simpering disclaimer, titled 'The Pen Points to Us'. Even so, you would expect enough sensitivity for *Outlook* not to commit at least in this issue the very offenses it charges the media with.

Shashi Tharoor, of all people, tells the media that political and world events matter more than affaires d'amour. In the thin guise of participating in a discussion on what is wrong with the media, he gets a forum to put up a comprehensive and uninterrupted defence against all the bad press he had. Conflict of interest?

Dipankar Gupta is a member of the News Broadcasting Standards Authority. Judge as prosecutor?

And as I turn page 57 I see a two-page spread titled "The Bhujbals. A Saga of leadership and vision." A eulogy to Chhagan Bhujbal and his two sons, it is the first of several such spreads, and nowhere does it say it is an ad. On the bottom left hand there is a logo that reads 'Outlook Spotlight'. Am I meant to know from that this is an ad? Or am I meant to think it isn't?

No doubt the intention was noble. But *Outlook* is after all very much part of the media it derides, and perhaps old habits die hard. So, rather like Julia in Byron's *Don Juan,*

> "A little still she strove,
>   and much repented,
> And whispering 'I will ne'er consent'
>   -- consented."

19

POLITICS, THEATRICS, AND THE ECONOMICS OF NEWS

If you have been professionally engaged with the news media from both within and without, it's hard not to comment, at this time, on their performance during the two-week Lokpal agitation.

In the newspapers the agitation was, understandably, the focus of the news, even if sometimes to the exclusion of what may otherwise have been front-page material.

Data for the specific period is not available but it is highly unlikely that readership and circulation were affected, since newspapers are sold almost entirely on subscription. In any case, given the relative stability of readership and six-monthly measurement, we will never know how readers responded. And as for advertising, it was business as usual.

---

[1] First published in *campaignindia.in,* Sep 2011

TV is a different animal altogether. Competitors keep an eye on each other and try to frantically outdo each other minute-to-minute, and the scorecard is out every week.

As the agitation progressed so did its share of airtime, even if there was often not much to report. It was not a situation that was unfolding rapidly, but 24X7 news is a voracious beast and has to be kept fed, even if like this:

> *Anchor: "The meeting is over, and Team Anna has headed back to Ramlila Ground, to report back to Anna Hazare and consult him on next steps. Let's go across to our reporter Mukul Bhatia, who is at Ground Zero. Mukul, what is the latest from Ramlila Ground?"*
>
> *Reporter: "Thank you, Neha. Yes, the atmosphere here is very charged. Team Anna represented by Kiran Bedi, Arvind Kejriwal and Prashant Bhushan has returned from its meeting with the Government. They have reached Ramlila Ground, and are now reporting back to Anna Hazare and consulting him on the next course of action. Our Political Editor Rahul Devdas has the inside story. Let's ask him for an update. Rahul, what can you tell us?"*

> *Political Editor: Thank you, Mukul. Yes, that's right. Team Anna has had a meeting with the Government. Team Anna was represented by Kiran Bedi, Arvind Kejriwal and Prashant Bhushan. We don't know yet exactly what transpired at the meeting, but what we do know is that they are now back at Ramlila Ground, where even as we speak they are reporting back to Anna Hazare and consulting him on the way forward. Mukul..."*

And so the day and the night wore on: agitated anchors wagging fingers at anyone in authority they could get in front of a camera; the same tired faces going over the same tired arguments, now on this channel, now on that; reporters filling time; and occasionally some real development worth reporting and discussing. TAM's News Content Track reports that on English and Hindi news channels the agitation took 83% of broadcast time in the second week.

At the end of the first week I remarked to the top Editor of a news channel that all of them were allowing no debate or discussion, just whipping up frenzy. He said, "In the beginning we were all fairly even handed. Then we realized this was where the audiences lay."

He was right. As the agitation helpfully started on a Monday and ended on a Saturday, we have a neat two weeks (34 and 35) of TAM data. Viewership of both English and Hindi news doubled from Week 33 (pre-agitation) to Week 34, and sustained in Week 35. The only other language in which news viewership grew was Marathi, by nearly 90% in Week 34.

Viewership in Telugu grew by 6% and 7% in those two weeks, but that was after 10% growth in the pre-agitation week, so doesn't seem related to the events of those weeks; and it actually declined in Tamil, Malayalam, Kannada, Bengali and Gujarati. If people in these areas were keeping up with the agitation, they were certainly not doing so on TV.

Meanwhile, advertising secondage in English and Hindi sustained in Week 34. Data for Week 35 is not available at the time of writing, but one news CEO confirmed what we saw, that they carried no ads in the second week. So while viewership doubled, revenue crashed.

That's the paradox of news TV: when news viewership is at its highest is the time when broadcasters earn no money. It is true that bad news sells. But while newspapers can happily carry ads in the midst of natural disasters, civil strife and war, it seems distasteful on TV to suddenly, in the midst of a distressing story, start talking about beautiful hair.

The frenetic, high-pitched tone typical of news channels in India is a business necessity. It's a bazaar out there. You have to shout and put on an act to get passing customers to stop at your stall instead of at your neighbour's.

The problem lies in the advertising-dependent business model. In the corrupt distribution system of TV, the household pays the cable operator, but the broadcaster doesn't get the money – or at best what the broadcaster does get is only a small fraction of what the household pays. This is the only business in which you pay for shelf space and provide the goods for free, and the shop owner earns from both you and your consumer.

At a fundamental level that is the problem of all media in India: that people don't pay for content. Leading newspapers are accused of the same thing that news TV is, of sensationalizing and trivializing the news. But they are leading because we buy them, and we buy them because of what they carry, much as we sanctimoniously criticize it. And because they sell more, they get more ads, and that is how they make money: the three rupees we pay don't cover even the cost of the forty pages of newsprint we get.

So if they have to be in business, they have to get ads; if they have to get ads, they have to chase eyeballs; and if they have to chase eyeballs, they have to do what gets the eyeballs. And until consumers pay for content or advertisers pay for quality rather than only quantity, that's how it is going to be.

"In the news market, you're not the customer but the product."

-- Yuval Noah Harari, in an interview to The Times of India, 2nd Sept 2018.

Excerpt from the interview:

"The struggle to capture people's attention has resulted in a destructive model for the news industry: 'exciting news that cost you nothing — in exchange for your attention'. Our attention is captured by sensational headlines, and is then sold to advertisers and politicians. In this battle for attention, there is little incentive to safeguard the truth.

"You might think that you are nevertheless getting a good bargain here. You don't have to pay anything, and you are entertained with interesting stories. But, in fact, you are not the customer at all, you are the product. You are being sold. You are giving up your most valuable asset — your attention — and you allow powerful corporations and politicians to brainwash you. That's crazy.

"A far better model for the news market would be 'high-quality news that cost you a lot of money, but does not abuse your attention'. If you are willing to pay for high-quality food, clothes and cars, why aren't you willing to pay for high-quality information?"

20

MEDIA OWNERSHIP: MORE QUESTIONS THAN ANSWERS

It used to be spoken of in whispers and written about obliquely; now it is reported openly. But the questions around big business investing in media remain.

About four months ago it was reported that Reliance would, in a typically complex transaction, invest Rs 1,500 crore in the companies that control Network 18 Media and TV18 Broadcast, two listed entities of TV18. To put that sum in perspective, at the time of reporting the two listed companies had a combined market cap of about Rs 1,800 crore. The deal will enable TV 18 to acquire the TV business of Eenadu, and make Reliance effectively the largest shareholder in TV 18.

Now it is reported that at least three big business houses are interested in acquiring 26% of TV Today. The Aditya Birla Group is reportedly the

---

[1] First published in *Impact*, April 2012

front-runner but denies any interest, which is of course standard practice. Market sources say Birla is expected to invest Rs 300-350 crore. Again, to put that in perspective, the market cap of TV Today at the time of writing is Rs 390 crore.

So what is the issue? These are diversified conglomerates, one may say, with interests in everything from shirts to cement and oil exploration to supermarkets, so why not in TV channels?

First of all, because you expect such conglomerates to go where the money is, but there is no money in the media business, and certainly not in broadcasting.

Of the touted Rs 72,800 crore Media & Entertainment sector in 2011 (*FICCI-KPMG*), Television accounts for Rs 32,900 crore, or 45%. The KPMG report does not give the composition of that, but the PwC report (*India Entertainment and Media Outlook*) of 2011 estimates the share of distribution to be 63%; of content providers, 4%; and of TV advertising – the sole source of net revenue for broadcasters – at 33%, which makes it just under Rs 11,000 crore in 2011. That's the *entire* television business, comprising, at last count, 623 channels: an average of Rs 18 crore per channel per year. That's less than half the cost of distribution for a medium-sized channel.

With the impending digitisation of cable the equations and the economics of the business are expected to change, in favour of broadcasters. That, perhaps, is the golden future big business is betting on. Well, if FICCI-KPMG estimates are to be believed, after full digitization in 2016 broadcasters will begin to get about a third of what consumers pay, against 10-15% now. Distribution will still get two-thirds.[2]

Small wonder that of the top ten media and entertainment companies by market cap on the BSE only five are in the television space, and three of those are pure play distribution companies – two of which belong to broadcasting networks.

In the present instance Network 18 is bleeding money from every pore while TV Today is barely profitable, with its revenue hovering around the same level for several years. Why would global scale, highly diversified, globally invested conglomerates with wide-open opportunities invest in a losing business in a bleeding sector?

If it is simply a desire to be in the media business – a perfectly legitimate desire – it is interesting that they go only into the news space,

---

[2] In fact, in 2018 broadcasters' share of distribution revenue was only 25%: Rs 11,000 crore of a total of Rs 43,500 crore. DPOs still got 75%. (EY: *A Billion Screens of Opportunity – India's Media & Entertainment Sector*, March 2019)

not into entertainment. A notable exception is Reliance ADAG's Big TV, which is apparently part of a larger, serious play in the cinema and entertainment space.[3]

The mainstream media have reported these developments, but briefly – and almost entirely without comment. No noisy TV debates, no editorial comment of note. The media don't write or talk about each other, and certainly not critically.

Rajya Sabha TV, lamentably little watched, did have a discussion featuring senior journalists and commentators – and not a good word to say on the matter. Madhu Trehan summed up the picture when she said, "When a politician or a government spokesman speaks, we don't believe them, but when somebody like Rajdeep Sardesai or Sagarika Ghosh speaks, or anyone at IBN7 or TV18 comes on, we presume we should believe them. Now there is a big question mark [when Reliance has indirect control over CNN-IBN].... We are looking at very subtle plants of stories, subtle angles, subtly putting things in a certain way so that people think in a certain way...."

While Trehan cited Reliance and TV 18 in the context, the principle obviously applies to any such situation. If there are some 15 news channels in Telugu, for instance, that cannot

---

[3] Reliance Big TV went out of business at the end of 2017.

be because it is a large and lucrative market. So there is really no difference, in principle, between Reliance buying control of TV 18 and a small businessman or a local politician owning a local news channel in Ranchi or Amritsar or Tiruchi. The difference is only of scale, and therefore of its potential to influence.

Many countries do regulate cross holding in media, with a view to preventing media monopolies. For all that, even in a highly regulated, media-rich country like the United States the media business is oligopolistic. In India the government tried about five years ago to bring in cross-holding legislation but had a huge fight on its hands, with both the political establishment and the media establishment waging all-out war against it, and ultimately shelved the draft bill.

The real issue in cross holding, to my mind, is not when a single company owns properties across print, TV and radio, but when a broadcasting network owns distribution channels. For a content owner to be in a position to control what gets to the viewer, and so be able to choke the pipeline for its competition, is a serious travesty of consumer rights. In India every major broadcasting network owns distribution platforms, and there is no law to protect the consumer[4].

While there is a modicum of action on other aspects of regulation, even if of questionable effectiveness, when it comes to regulating who may invest in media at all there is little or no legislation in the free world, nor does it appear practical. It does seem, on the face of it, well nigh impossible, in a free-market democracy, to stop anyone from owning anything unless it is established that such ownership distorts the free market.

If you can't regulate the ownership of media, can you regulate its use, or misuse?

Even regulation of content is a fraught issue. The Press Council of India is famously toothless, made no better by its present Chairman, "who is baiting the media, who doesn't believe in conversing with the media," as S Nihal Singh says. The News Broadcasters Association took a laudable initiative in self-regulation, but the effectiveness of the mechanism is debatable and indeed frequently debated. The Indian Broadcasting Foundation, after squirming and obfuscating for years, finally set up a mechanism, but it is too early to say how – even if – it works.

---

[4] Star TV is now the exception. Since its acquisition by The Walt Disney Company it has no distribution interests in India.

Any discussion on regulation – of ownership; of cross holding; or of content – runs into questions of freedom of speech and raises constitutional issues; and the hallowed Article 19 is invoked, and with good reason. Now the Supreme Court has asked what can be done if business entities use the media to harass rivals, what mechanism is available to deal with such a situation. In response counsel for the media said – predictably, but not wrongly – that the court can do whatever is in its power, but not at the cost of the right to free speech.

Dilip Cherian holds out no hope for media legislation in India, citing the nexus between business and politics. "As a country we are not able to legislate for two reasons," he said on Rajya Sabha TV. "One, because of the influence big business houses have on policy making. And two, when you bring legislation (on regulation) up, the other group that is affected are the politicians who own media houses of their own. You are talking about a new coalition of forces which the public is incapable of handling."

Where we are today is far from perfect, but every solution raises its own problems. Big business must not be allowed to control the media, but who wants a fragmented, anarchic melee of small, unaccountable media? Media monopolies are unhealthy, but do you trust the government to decide who can own what? Self-regulation of content is not working; but do you want the government to decide what we should see and read?

It's a complex web of issues. Where we are today is the outcome of conflicting forces and vested interests playing out over many years. It's like global warming: it affects my life in fundamental ways; its effect is not dramatic today but its potential to damage is huge; and I don't have a cogent solution, but I know it is something I have to be concerned about.

21

CAN'T IMAGINE WHAT THEY WERE THINKING

The closure of *Imagine* brought two questions to mind. Why now? And why would they have expected a different outcome?

In the space of about eight months in 2007-08 the Hindi GEC space saw the high-profile launches of four channels. The best thing that can be said about *Real* is that its owners didn't dawdle in applying the guillotine. 9X had a chequered life, but at least it served the useful purpose of enabling its promoter to keep himself in golf balls and single malt in the English countryside for the rest of his life[2].

Imagine was launched by NDTV in early 2008, opening with 56 GRPs (CS 4+, HSM), and taken over by Turner at the end of 2009. Twelve

---

[1]   First published in *Impact*, May 2012.
[2]   That comment about the promoter of 9X was made in jest, long before the unfortunate events that overtook him. I know that at the time he would have had a good laugh about it. I have chosen not to edit it.

weeks into Turner's tenure (Week 10 of 2010) viewership peaked at 176 GRPs, and then went quite steadily downhill for the next two years, getting back where it started – 54 GRPs – in the week before its closure was announced.

It was not just Turner, the short history of *Real* notwithstanding: *Imagine* never had a chance. It started with the fairly fail-proof offering of *Ramayana* but ran soaps in weekly episodes, harking back to the old *Doordarshan* format for an audience that had become used to daily soaps. Why they thought that was a good idea shall remain a mystery, the more so because Sameer Nair, then CEO, was famously the one responsible for moving Star Plus from weekly to daily soaps, with great success. The only apparent reason seems to be economy: making each episode last seven days instead of one.

They did move to daily soaps in 2009 and saw a blip in viewership, but soon went on to reality programming of a type, like *Rakhi ka Swayamvar*, the Rahul Mahajan show and a couple of other such faintly disreputable shows. Originality is a good thing but not, for a mass market offering, if it doesn't appeal to the core consumer. *Imagine* did get some traction, but its viewers were not the mainstream audience that makes GEC prime time what it is. It also ran rather quickly out of steam and went into repetitions *ad nauseum.*

Colors launched in Week 30, opening at the same level as *Imagine* was in the same week, its twenty-sixth. Then rapidly building and maintaining three to four times the size of viewership, it has stayed consistently among the top four in the genre, alongside the three legacy channels, week after week.

The question, of course, is what has made *Colors* different from its late, unlamented contemporaries.

What you have to do depends on the scale of your ambition, which in the case of *Colors* was clearly to be in the big league. In a crowded category with well-entrenched leaders, you don't do that by ingratiating yourself over time: you break the door down and barge in, in one fell swoop. No one is looking for another TV channel. You have to break into their consciousness; intrigue them enough to make them want to check it out; be available right alongside the channels you want to pull them away from, not expect them to search for you; and then, when they do sample your fare, be liked enough for them to want to keep coming back.

Colors pulled out the stops in product, distribution and promotion. It started with big shows, upped the ante on distribution – the broadcasting industry was agog with whispers about how much they spent – and invested heavily in advertising and promotion. It's not only a matter of having the resources; it is a matter of having the risk appetite to put money, careers and reputations on the line, and then the energy to fight every single day to keep your place at the top table.

It's true that in marketing nothing succeeds like success, and nothing fails like failure. Success and failure are fluently explained after the event, but the question is, what were you thinking when you launched or acquired the brand? In the cold light of day, what did you think you were doing that would induce consumers to exercise their choices in your favour? That is all marketing is: inducing people to exercise their choices in your favour. And that's the one question to which top management must have the answer. That's the difference between success and failure. The rest is detail.

22

THE TAM HAS COME...

> *"The time has come," the Walrus said,*
> *"To talk of many things:*
> *Of shoes - and ships - and sealing-wax -*
> *Of cabbages - and kings."*
>   -- *Lewis Carroll* Through
>   the Looking Glass

First, a disclaimer: I hold no brief for TAM, or for any company or industry body. Also, I have no knowledge of the alleged corruption in the TAM system, and neither am competent to comment on it nor wish to.

In all that is being said about the ills of the audience measurement system, a lot remains unsaid, as broadcasters and other stakeholders look over their shoulders when they speak. Having led broadcast networks as well as media agencies and been in the leadership of industry bodies, I too have debated the issues and heard the arguments. But I have no skin in the game anymore, so I don't need to be circumspect.

---

[1] First published in *agencyfaqs.com*, Aug 2012

The rumblings began, or at least became audible, in 2005, when MRUC called meetings of advertisers, broadcasters and agencies in Mumbai and Delhi, and initiated discussion on the shortcomings of TAM. But these were only crib sessions: they proposed no action plan. Much heat was generated; rhetoric indulged in; tea and samosas consumed; and everyone went back to business as usual, crunching TAM data to do media plans and deals.

I said it then and I say it now: if the industry is a victim, it is a complicit victim.

That TAM is inadequate for the current context and marketplace is perhaps inarguable. But broadcasters and agencies have been using data that they say is inadequate and inaccurate at best, and manipulated at worst, to further their business: to direct the spending of clients' money. That is over Rs 60,000 crore of TV ad expenditure in the seven years since 2005, when MRUC initiated the discussion (basis: PwC estimates). That this is the only data available is no argument: that's like saying, "I know I'm lying: but I don't know the truth, so let's go with the lie." So who is the victim? The advertiser, I should think.

The biggest point of contention has always been the sample size, and everyone has their own prescription. I am no market researcher or statistician, so I cannot comment on what the sample size should be, but it is clear that currently it is inadequate for the large and complex market that India is.

TAM as we know it was the result of the merger of two systems: TAM and INTAM. They were created at a time when the media world was simpler. The big advertisers were FMCG marketers; most brands addressed females in the age group of 15-44 years; and most programming was entertainment. In that simple world, TAM as a broad measure was perhaps adequate. As channels and genres of content proliferated, audiences got fragmented and newer categories began to be advertised, addressed to other, more sharply defined audiences. The need for finer measurement grew but the system remained the same, buffered now and then by some increase in sample.

And what did the users do? Sliced and diced the data at will, ignoring the fact that they were dealing in dangerously small samples.

Broadcasters use TAM data not only to negotiate and sell specific deals to advertisers and agencies, but to advertise themselves, too. Every news channel runs ads claiming to be No.1, on some day and time of its choosing. And they do worse than split hairs. Consider the fact that English news has, on an average, 0.1 per cent share of total TV viewership. If a channel with 23 per cent share claims to be the leader because it has a two-percentage point lead over the next one, that's a difference of 2 per cent of 0.1 per cent of TV viewership - based on a notoriously inadequate sample.

Is English news viewership really so tiny? Perhaps it isn't. Perhaps this is a reflection of the inadequacy of TAM. But you can't use the data to show off your prowess, on the one hand, and question its veracity, on the other.

There have often been discussions, formal and informal, with TAM and among user bodies, on the need to increase the sample. The problem is no one wants to pay more than they already are, though they want more than they are getting.

About a year ago, the NBA demanded that TAM release news viewership data monthly instead of weekly. They somehow positioned this as being in the public interest, and mustered government support for it. Thankfully, the idea sank - under the weight of its own sheer ludicrousness, perhaps.

In March 2012 at FICCI Frames was announced, amid much applause, the formation of the Broadcast Audience Research Council (BARC). An industry initiative to develop a robust, user-driven audience measurement system, BARC brings together the industry bodies of the three key stakeholders: broadcasters (IBF), advertisers (ISA) and advertising agencies (AAAI). Part of the announcement at Frames was the much-lauded bringing aboard of the AAAI, by the other two.

At last, a welcome step in the right direction? Yes, except that the three bodies first met about six years ago, and in time formed BARC as an equal three-way partnership. Nothing seems to have happened after that except that two years ago AAAI was thrown out, for reasons that remain unclear. And nothing seems to have happened since, except the announcement at Frames and, subsequently, IBF accusing its 'partners' of delaying the process.

So it appears, sadly, that the industry bodies of the three stakeholders cannot together find a solution to their single biggest collective problem. Finding fault is not enough. Either manage the current system or change it. Now.

At the time this piece was written TAM was under fire and BARC, which had been in formation for four years by then, was moving in fits and starts. At the end of 2012 TAM set up the TAM Transparency Panel, an international group of independent experts, as an ombudsman body for TV ratings, on which I served. BARC has since replaced TAM as the ratings provider, and has its own set of issues. See p. 136, The New TV Ratings System has Drawbacks, Too.

23

MEDIA REGULATION: BETWEEN THE DEVIL AND THE DEEP SEA

Observer Research Foundation, a New Delhi-based think tank, held a seminar on Perspectives in Media Regulation: Lessons from the UK, *with featured speakers from the Reuters Institute for the Study of Journalism, London. The question, as always, is, can we effectively regulate media in India? Indeed, should the media be regulated? By whom?*

The on-going debate on media regulation is in many ways the stuff of the coffee house debates of the sixties, in which *jhola*-carrying intellectuals diagnosed the ills of the world and prescribed remedies, while the rest carried on running the world in their own ham-handed way.

---

[1] First published in *mxmindia.com*, Feb 2014

Perhaps the best indication of this, at last week's seminar, was in the presence – or otherwise – of a member of the broadcast regulatory body, TRAI. The hosts indicated their seriousness by having Dr Vijaylakshmi Gupta give the keynote address, obviously to set the Indian context before we heard about the UK. Dr Gupta indicated hers by reading out a prepared, platitudinous speech and leaving immediately.

And so the coffee house debate carries on....

In a discussion on regulation on another occasion I wondered why the media have a say in whether they wish to be regulated: were the banking, or insurance, or telecoms or airline companies asked if they do? The Chairman of the News Broadcasting Standards Authority answered that was because the media sector is special, not like any ordinary business, and has a role of national importance. Unlike banks and insurance and...?

If you break the broad regulation issue into its component parts, it comes down to two distinct aspects: ownership and content. Issues of ownership include both, the *who?* question- who should own the media; and the *what?* question – what they should be allowed to own, i.e., cross-media ownership.

The ownership question has no real answers. The discussion at another seminar a few weeks ago was perhaps typical. A senior journalist, who had recently had a fairly public falling-out with his corporate employers, was critical of non-media corporates owning media companies. He was also not in favour of media conglomerates; owner-editors; journalist-owners; and of government or political parties owning media. I said I couldn't disagree with what he had said, and asked who then, in his opinion, should own the media. No answer.

The point is not to find fault with this speaker. It is, rather, that this is an unresolvable issue, in which every answer raises fresh questions. What is necessary is not to limit who may and who may not own, but transparency about who does. It calls, as with most things in India, not necessarily for new regulations but first for implementing existing regulations.

The other aspect of the ownership question is cross-media holding: born of the concern that media conglomerates, through cross-media domination, can drive public opinion. That's a theoretically sound concern, but in practice doubtful at two levels. First, it is questionable whether in the pluralistic environment that is India even the largest media conglomerate can actually drive public opinion.

Second, what is the efficacy of such regulation? Even in the highly regulated and media-rich United States the media business is oligopolistic.

And yet, going back to the first question, it is doubtful if any of the six dominant houses is in a position to actually drive public opinion.

The real issue in cross holding is not, to my mind, when a single company owns properties across print, TV, radio and the Internet, but when a broadcasting network owns distribution channels. For a content owner to be in a position to control what gets to the viewer, and so be able to choke the pipeline for its competition, is a serious travesty of consumer rights. In India every major broadcasting network owns distribution platforms[2], the two biggest networks have collaborated in a joint venture to distribute content, and there is no law to protect the consumer. That is a serious issue for the regulatory authorities to address. [3]

---

[2]   This was entirely true at the time of writing but now Star TV, since its 2018 acquisition by The Walt Disney Company, has no distribution interests.

[3]   At the time of writing content aggregation was a thriving business, dominating both small networks and standalone channels, on the one side, and distribution platforms (cable and DTH), on the other. The Star and Zee networks were operating a joint venture company that was a content aggregator, so the two biggest networks in the country were combining their might to jointly negotiate terms with distribution platforms. TV18 had its own content aggregation company, which also had other broadcasters for clients. In Feb 2014 (on the day this piece was first published, in fact) the TRAI announced new regulations and brought an end to the practice of content aggregators.

The real, vexed question is of content regulation. Can we? Indeed, should we? Self-regulation or statutory? And, all the while, a government that has been trying for five years to regulate audience measurement wants you to believe that it is committed to self-regulation in content. It is the same government that in its previous term tried to create a broadcast regulator who would be not a constitutional authority but be hired and fired by the government. The proposed structure also required each broadcaster to have on its rolls a Content Auditor who would screen content and tell the Editor what to drop or modify and – incredibly – inform the broadcast regulator if the Editor didn't comply.

The UK currently has no regulation of print media. The response of the press to the Leveson enquiry and the consequent government proposal is to resist any regulatory mechanism, which is to be expected. But it must be said, in fairness, that the News of the World scandal, though huge, was a 'rarest of the rare' case that was effectively exposed and dealt with swiftly, which is a great deal more than we can expect. Whether one NOTW should lead from no regulation to statutory regulation is debatable.

In the US, too, there is no regulatory mechanism – self- or government. It depends entirely on good practice. The Editor is responsible, and owners typically take a back seat on editorial decisions. Would an editor carry content prejudicial to the owner's interests? Probably not, but in a robust media environment you can't stop the rest of the world from seeing you.

In India broadcasters, in particular, have made moves to self-regulation by setting up the News Broadcasting Standards Authority (NBSA) and, for entertainment content, the Broadcast Content Complaints Council, both under the aegis of the broadcast industry bodies. An inherent limitation of such self-regulation is that it is limited to the members of these bodies. In the case of news that means 53 channels of 23 NBA member broadcasters[4]. The other 150 known news broadcasters in the country are beyond the pale.

The effectiveness of self-regulation is often questioned because, even if you don't doubt their intent, self-regulatory bodies do not have the statutory authority to penalise offenders. Members themselves often don't accept the rulings of the regulators they have created. Indeed, the first time the NBSA indicted a broadcaster the peeved member quit the NBA in protest.

Dr David Levy of the Reuters Institute had an interesting take on the matter. He said effectiveness of self-regulation is a function first of culture, far more than of legal guarantees.

---

[4] Now 70 channels of 27 members. (Source: NBA website)

In other words, some of us are made that way, and some just aren't. The implication that we are incapable of self-regulation may raise some hackles but, let's face it, that's fundamentally true.

The very idea of statutory regulation, on the other hand, is anathema. Those of us of a certain age have actually lived through it in its extreme form, nearly 40 years ago, and can't begin to contemplate what it might be like in this multimedia age.

So where does that leave us, between the devil and the deep sea?

Giving statutory penal authority to self-regulatory bodies has its own set of issues. The only viable answer seems to be co-regulation. I see a system in which a self-regulatory body such as the NBSA conveys a verdict and recommends a penalty to a statutorily authorised one, such as perhaps the TRAI. If the statutory body does not agree with the recommendation, it must respond to the recommending body through a laid-down process, and the two come to an agreement.

That media owners protest against any and all forms of regulation is not surprising: who wants to be regulated? Every time content is mentioned in the same breath as regulation, even a limit on advertising time, they get all excited about

Article 19, freedom of speech, democracy, *et al.* While no one doubts the sanctity of our constitutional freedoms, there can be no such thing as unfettered freedom. The trouble is, the press think everyone should be accountable and subject to criticism and control – the legislature, the executive and the judiciary; indeed, both Church and State – except themselves.

There is no perfect solution. The best is one that protects consumer interest, and that necessarily means some measure of control while enabling and protecting media freedom.

24

SO WHERE SHOULD THE MONEY COME FROM?

> *TRAI's Recommendations on Issues Relating to Media Ownership, its second on the subject, is in the familiar TRAI mould: well presented, articulate, easy-to-read, and theoretically sound, but often opinionated, self-righteous and of questionable practicality.*

That there are serious issues relating to ownership is without doubt, and the *de facto* acquisition of Network 18 by Reliance has thrown many of them up in stark relief. Even if there is no end in sight, they are important enough

---

[1] First published in Aug 2014 in *thehoot.org*, then an independent media watch website. The Hoot Archive is now hosted by Ashoka Archives, the Archives of Contemporary India project at Ashoka University, for archiving and preserving primary source material for the study of the modern and contemporary history of India.

to discuss periodically, in the expectation that some resolution will evolve over time.

While some have questioned the parameters set by the regulator, it seems sensible to limit the subject for the present as proposed, to where it is most relevant: news and current affairs; on print and TV only; and with markets defined by language-state combination.

That said, it is in the main a one-sided view, lacking the very internal plurality it champions. A comprehensive review of it could be longer than the document itself, so I will confine myself to a few salient aspects.

Whose money is it, anyway?

At a seminar some months ago a senior journalist, who had recently had a public falling-out with his corporate employers, was critical of non-media corporates owning media companies. He was also not in favour of media conglomerates; owner-editors; journalist-owners; and of government or political parties owning media. I asked who then, in his opinion, should own the media. No answer.

The point is not to find fault with that journalist. It is, rather, that this is a fraught issue, in which every answer raises fresh questions. What is necessary is not to limit who may and who may not own, but transparency about who does. It calls, as with most things in India, not necessarily for new regulations but first for implementing existing ones.

No doubt *"the mission of the news media is not to promote the advertiser's interest by facilitating 'consumption' but to promote the citizens' interest by facilitating unbiased dissemination of information"*. Nice rhetoric, but where does the money come from? Surely the regulator is aware of the economics of the media business, especially of broadcasting, which is its remit. Surely, too, the regulator is aware that broadcasters still don't get the benefits of digitization because the intractable last mile does not implement the mandated subscriber management systems, and no one – not TRAI, not the I&B Ministry – has been able to make LCOs (local cable operators) comply. (That is why now, on 23rd August, the government has pushed the digitization deadline by a year.)

As long as people don't pay for content, advertising will remain the lifeblood of the media business. And as long as all their revenue comes from advertisers, that is who they will cater to. Do they have an option?

A news channel selling advertisements, and ensuring its ability to do so, is like a man who works long hours and has little time for his family. His mission is to provide for the well being of his family, but it's the job that gives him the resources to do that. Stop whipping him for spending all his time at work: instead, ensure he is paid well enough; control inflation; and make quality education and healthcare affordable. Trust me, he would rather be free.

Sound and fury about private treaties

The near obsession with Private Treaties is out of proportion with the significance of the phenomenon and, if it is indeed significant, with the possibility of doing anything meaningful about it.

This is a line of business in which a media owner has small stakes in multiple companies. Is that a bigger problem than corporate ownership? And what about the influence of big advertisers? Does anyone know what proportion of revenue comes from so-called private treaties deals? And if indeed it is big issue, has anyone got the media owners' perspective on it?

Private treaties "*could be in various forms,*" the document irresponsibly speculates, "*such as advertising in exchange for equity of the advertising company or in exchange for favourable coverage. They could also take the form of giving favourable coverage to companies in exchange for exclusive advertising rights. Other innovative forms of private treaties could also exist.*" Such speculation is out of place in a document of this nature. Surely it is the duty of an authority recommending a policy to do its homework; and surely TRAI has the wherewithal to get the necessary information.

And here is clinching proof offered, of skullduggery: *"During the 2008 recession, these media entities refused to admit that the recession had indeed hit the country and instead called it a 'temporary slowdown' in order to prevent the stock prices of the companies they owned and companies that owned them from falling; else they were likely to lose big money."*

That is perhaps the single most ridiculous statement in the entire 111-page document. Did the Government of India or the Reserve Bank say it was a recession? Didn't they, on the contrary, actually insist it was only a slowdown? So did the Finance Minister, too, refuse to admit it was a recession because he risked losing big money? Would it have been better if the media had cried itself hoarse and caused panic, and the markets had crashed?

The simplistic, one-word recommendation to "proscribe" private treaties seems to give little thought to the practicality of such a measure. Does it mean media houses cannot invest in companies, or that their owners cannot? Does it mean they cannot carry perfectly legitimate advertisements of companies they have perfectly legitimate investments in? Does it mean their rate negotiations will be subject to approval by some authority?

Regulation, Self-regulation, Co-regulation

NBSA is dismissed lightly because its standards apply only to the 57 channels of 28 NBA members[2].

Sadly, there is no informed assessment of it, or a word of appreciation for the fact that these broadcasters have taken the initiative. Instead, the Authority dismisses it as an *"ineffective regulatory framework"* and only quotes an unnamed organisation that has moved the Supreme Court against it, describing it as *"a self-serving farce".*

The Authority further betrays its bias when, in answering the question, *"Has self-regulation worked?"* it begins disdainfully with, *"The cosy club mentality of this mechanism…."* That is hardly calculated to give the confidence of the objective assessment that is the bounden duty of a regulator.

In fact, the entire concept of self-regulation has been dismissed, simply because it is a voluntary act. There is not a single reference to, not a single attempt to give, the perspective of the NBSA, of its Chairman, who is a retired Chief

---

[2] Now 70 channels of 27 members. (Source: NBA website)

Justice of India, or of editors and broadcast executives – only of their detractors.

It is fair to have expected the Authority to first assess the NBSA mechanism and then address the question of what next, and weigh options. What it has done, instead, is to point out the issues of statutory regulation and then go on to recommend it anyway, under the aegis of a Media Regulator. It does not make the critical distinction between content and structural regulation: statutory content regulation can easily become censorship; structural regulation is essential for fair competition.

There are two key issues with self-regulation. The first is its limited applicability: in the case of NBSA, only to NBA members. The answer to that is to mandatorily bring all news channels under the jurisdiction of the NBSA.

The second issue is that penalties imposed by self-regulatory bodies are not enforceable, but giving penal authority to self-regulatory bodies has its own set of issues. The only viable answer is co-regulation, in which a self-regulatory body such as NBSA conveys a verdict and a proposed penalty to a statutorily empowered one, such as perhaps the proposed Media Regulator. The statutory body either accepts and implements the recommendation or reviews and modifies it. How hard is that?

Guilty until proven innocent

What is most galling throughout the document is the disdain towards every link in the media value chain. The best that can be said is that it is equal-opportunity disdain: everyone is tarred with the same brush. The only sources and views cited are those that support the Authority's agenda. No alternative views are presented.

It is no one's case that all is well with the news media. Everyone knows about motivated ownership, and indeed the document describes the issues in detail. But indicting the entire industry and practically all its constituents is unacceptable. The least an industry can expect of its regulator is even-handedness, and that is regrettably lacking.

25

THE NEW TV RATINGS SYSTEM HAS DRAWBACKS, TOO

The transition from TAM (Television Audience Measurement) to the BARC (Broadcast Audience Research Council) TV ratings system was a period of significant upheaval in the broadcasting business and its lifeblood, which is advertising. In April 2015 BARC began to deliver data, amid much uncertainty. The Hoot sought my views on some of the many questions about BARC.

BARC is here. Does that take us closer to a more satisfactory audience measurement system than TAM, in your view? And if not why not?

That BARC – or any vendor – is here cannot be an assurance of anything. The proof of the pudding is in the eating.

---

[1] First published in *thehoot.org*, May 2015

Do you see any improvement over TAM ratings in the metrics that the new measurement system has produced so far?

So far, no: mainly because this is household level data. What that means is, BARC data as of now tells you only what a household is tuned into: not who in the household is watching. That's of precious little use in media planning and buying. It is okay for testing the system and settling it down, but viewer level data is the table stakes. Until you have that you aren't in the game. So for the purpose of media planning and buying BARC data is not yet useful.

Will BARC be able to deliver better value to advertisers and media planners?

In principle there is no reason why it shouldn't. But my concern as an industry observer, and one who has been deeply involved with the subject, is that this measurement system is controlled by those who are being measured.

BARC was intended to be an equal-stakes venture of three industry bodies[2]. But finally broadcasters have 60% of the vote, while the other two constituents have only 20% each. In effect, those whose performance is being

---

[2] The Indian Broadcasting Foundation (IBF); the Indian Society of Advertisers (ISA); and the Advertising Agencies Association of India (AAA of I)

measured hold sway: they don't need the support of the others to do pretty much anything.

BARC was set up because the industry decided it didn't want a vendor-driven system. It has traded that for a broadcaster-driven system. How that is better is for the other two constituents – advertisers and their media agencies – to judge.

What are the implications and advantages of watermarking?

I'm not qualified to compare technologies, but there are two limitations I'm aware of.

One, the broadcaster controls the switch. If you're disgruntled and don't want your channel to be measured you can simply stop watermarking, and the system will not be able to read your channel[3]. That is not good. It will distort the picture. If I am doing market research on shampoo, for example, and am asking sample homes which brand of shampoo they use, I don't want Brand X deciding that it won't allow its consumers to reveal themselves. A major network doing that could hold the whole system to ransom.

Two, it is expensive. Small, single-channel broadcasters, of whom there are hundreds, will find it hard to afford. Other technologies don't

---

[3] This is exactly what happened two years later. See page 170, *NBA vs Republic TV -- the Pot Calling the Kettle...?*

require anything of the broadcaster. So it could result in a partial picture, with data only for participating channels.

The universe from which the sample was chosen is the same as MRUC's IRS. Is this a satisfactory universe, and if not why not?

Considering the question mark that hangs over the IRS, I would worry about it.

The sampling is 20,000 households going to 50,000 in four years. Do you think that the sample will be sufficiently scientifically chosen to represent 160 million households satisfactorily? It is just double the earlier sampling TAM did, which was pretty small.

First, the question of sample size. We are always concerned about sample size, perhaps because that is easy to grasp.

People generally think what matters is the relationship between the size of the universe and that of the panel. That seems reasonable, but statisticians will tell you that a panel of 10,000 correctly representative of its universe will be as good a measure whether the universe is, say, 10 million or a billion. What matters is not the relationship between the size of the panel and the size of the universe but that between the size of the panel and the smallness of what it is trying to measure.

When TV audience measurement started in this country the media world was relatively simple. There were few channels; TV was mainly entertainment; the most advertised products were fmcg, mostly targeted at women, 15-44, SEC A-C. That was a broad measure, for which the then sample of perhaps 4-5,000 homes was adequate.

Over time not only the number but the genres of TV channels grew; the range of advertised product categories widened to include financial services, auto, mobile telephones, consumer durables, ... and, correspondingly, the audiences targeted began to include different demographics. So now you were measuring smaller and smaller channels, in relation to more finely defined audiences.

And the TAM sample grew, too. Decision point: as you add more homes, should you cover more towns or increase the sample size in current towns, i.e., cover more towns thinly or cover fewer towns in depth? That depends on what you seek to achieve. I remember when news broadcasters asked TAM not to increase the geographical spread of its sample because more towns covered would mean more carriage fees.

Of course you can increase the sample in both width and depth of coverage, but someone has to pay for it. There's no free lunch.

Second, BARC is starting with 20,000 meters, representing all markets. 70% of the meters will be urban: that's 14,000 meters representing 71 million urban TV households spread across more towns and further down pop strata, compared with TAM's 10,000 meters representing 61 million in Class 1+ pop strata.

BARC will also represent 82 million rural households with 6,000 meters. If sample size is an issue, how can that be even remotely representative of a universe as culturally diverse and geographically dispersed as rural India?

Yes, it is meant to go up to 50,000 meters over time. But that's an intention, and eventually someone has to pay for it. If they do, and if it happens, wonderful.

But, as I said, it's not just about the sample size: that's simply the easiest handle to grab.

BARC will be using the National Consumer Classification System instead of the socio-economic one. Please explain this and tell us what its advantage is?

The Socio-Economic Classification (SEC) system came about in the late 1980's on the initiative of the Market Research Society of India (MRSI). The object was to find a better predictor of consumption behaviour than household income, which was commonly used until then. The reason is obvious: two households with similar incomes don't necessarily behave alike with respect to consumption. So what is it about them that most influences consumption behaviour?

The MRSI did research to determine which parameters best indicated a household's propensity to consume, and concluded that it was a combination of the education and occupation of the chief wage earner (CWE).

That made sense intuitively, too.

The SEC was adopted starting with the National Readership Survey (NRS) of 1988. Some 12 or 15 years later users began to question its relevance, and the Media Research Users Council (MRUC) began to consider a new SEC structure. In 2011 MRUC and MRSI introduced the new system, the NCCS.

The NCCS is also based on two parameters, one of which is the education of the CWE. The other is not occupation, as it was earlier, but the number of durables owned by the household, from a list of 11.

There are all kinds of analyses to show why and how the NCCS is better. But to my mind it is terribly left-brained, the work of technocrats. If the purpose is to classify households according to their *propensity* to consume, we must look for indicators of their *likely behaviour*. Ownership of durables is manifest behaviour: they consume lots, so they must have a high propensity to consume.

The SEC system is more stable. For a household those parameters change slowly over time, and if they do change then that's a result of a life change, or results in a life change. If the CWE has acquired more education or upgraded their occupation that will definitely lead to a higher propensity to consume, so their SEC should change.

In the NCCS, on the other hand, if a household that owns one durable today were to buy two more next year its classification would change. Over time all households will own more durables, so everyone's classification will change.[4] That doesn't make sense to me.

---

[4] The proportion of SECs (or NCCS categories) has been changing exactly as I expected, with households moving up the ladder. The Broadcast India (BI) survey 2016 reported that D and E households together accounted for 44% of the universe; in the BI 2018 report they are down to 38%. Meanwhile each edition of the Indian Readership Survey (IRS) reports that NCCS D/E is on a continuous decline – going from 54.5% of the universe reported in IRS 2013 to 35.4% in IRS Q2 2019. This is supported by data for consumer durables, which show predictable increases in penetration of durables like ceiling fans, gas stoves, colour TVs, two-wheelers and refrigerators. That is eminently desirable from the standpoint of economic growth, but does not make for a stable discriminating variable.

Do you think that the fact that BARC segregates the functions of data collection, analysis and reporting between three independent agencies will make it less prone to misuse and lead to more dependable metrics?

The practice is not unique. It is followed elsewhere in the world, too. There's no single right way to do things. In the end what matters is panel and data security. The biggest problem is not misuse of the reported data: it's before the data is reported, i.e., panel tampering, so the fewer the people or agencies involved in that process, the better.

In the end everything can be violated if you have a mind to: think of 9/11; think of 26/11. We can only try; and we can take deterrent action against those who are caught, to discourage stray thoughts in that direction.

The expectation is that a better designed system with more sampling will lead to news broadcasters at least reducing sensationalism and being less driven by one big eyeball grabbing story. Is that a realistic expectation?

I'm afraid not. News broadcasters do what they do not because the measurement system is imperfect but because that's what they do. Do you think Times Now will be quite happy to show up as no. 2 to CNN-IBN because – thank God! – we at last have a sensible measurement system? They will continue to push frenetically to maximize their score, whatever the scoring system[5].

What is the sense you are getting of the industry response so far to BARC – from broadcasters, advertisers and advertising agencies who are all represented in it ownership? Or is it too early to tell?

It's too early to tell.

So far the advertisers and advertising agencies are playing ball. The advertisers have agreed to do without data until BARC is able to supply it. They spent huge sums on the IPL after planning with individual-level TAM data, and are evaluating it either with household-level BARC data; or with the previous season's TAM data; or not at all. That's amazing.

I can't imagine what's motivating them, but evidently getting BARC going is important enough to them to risk hundreds of crore of their advertising money shooting in the dark at a moving target.

---

[5] When Arnab Goswami, then Editor-in-Chief of *Times Now*, saw this he told me, "You're certainly right about *Times Now*!"

26

LIKE THE CURATE'S EGG: GOOD IN PARTS

Book Review

Behind a Billion Screens, by Nalin Mehta (New Delhi: Harper Collins India, April 2015)

Nalin Mehta has been an academician and a journalist. This book has been researched by the academician and written by the journalist.

The academician is most evident in the extensive, painstaking annotation: 53 pages of endnotes to support 221 pages of text. The early account of the ills that plague news television is sound, balanced and pragmatic, and later in the book Mehta presents an excellent historical perspective of broadcast regulation in India, right up to the present day. The detailed exposition of self-regulation is also well informed and instructive, and makes a good

---

[1] First published in *thehoot.org*, Jul 2015

and valid comparison of the functioning of the two bodies, the News Broadcast Standards Authority for news and the Broadcast Content Complaints Council for entertainment. For all this the book is a must for anyone concerned with – and about – the management of television broadcasting in India.

But the journalist in Mehta is irrepressible, and dominates the discourse. That would be no issue, if this were not a journalist with an agenda, characterised by sweeping statements, sometimes bordering on the irresponsible; specious use of data; and ignoring inconvenient facts to make a point. The 10-page introduction by Uday Shankar, CEO of Star TV, sets the tone: the book goes on to represent Star TV's world view, with Shankar extensively quoted and frequently referred to throughout, and numerous examples cited of Star's bold, innovative, far-sighted moves worthy of a leader.

Speaking of news TV ownership and describing in some detail how Zee built its news network, on the other hand, Mehta comments that, "Zee's business moves were not ideological." That may well be true, but not a mention is made of the origins of Star News – the sweetheart deal with NDTV and the split; the attempt to structure a company with Vir Sanghvi, Suhel Seth, *et al*; how it ended up with ABP; and how Star News became ABP News, whereby hangs a tale.

The author is at pains to establish that the big TV networks are not as big as we might think, and asserts that they are disadvantaged with respect to buyers of advertising time. "70% of all media expenditure in India is controlled by only five media groups.... On the sellers' side, however, fragmentation rules. There are more than 800 TV channels...." The numbers hide more than they reveal, as is often the case. What we are not told is that the Big 5 are present and strong across all genres of TV, and bundle their weak properties with the strong ones (and why shouldn't they?), so that ultimately the two sides, buyers and sellers, are ranged across the table as countervailing forces. There's nothing wrong with that, but the point is that the big networks are quite well, thank you very much: it's the long tail of hundreds of small and stand-alone broadcasters that continues to writhe in agony.

On the subject of distribution, and of digitisation, Mehta seems confused. Citing unattributed data, he says that in the period 2005-11 distribution costs more than tripled but subscription revenue barely increased, with the result that "the net money that channels made from subscriptions in this period actually reduced by almost half". That's amusing, because it means broadcasters were, or are, net earners from subscription. Here are the facts.

Of 832 'permitted' satellite channels in the country some 250 are pay channels. The rest, being free-to-air, only pay carriage fees: they earn no subscription revenue. Of the 250 that do, about 140 belong, directly or indirectly, to the Big 5 networks, and they (fewer than 20% of the total) are the ones who are net earners from subscription. For the rest subscription revenue only subsidises their distribution cost. Not much for the big boys to complain about.

One of the reasons why the big networks are net earners is of course that they own properties no cable operator can afford not to carry. The other is that they themselves have distribution interests: each of them owns and influences, directly or indirectly, every link in the distribution value chain: content aggregators; multi-system operators (MSOs); local cable operators (LCOs); and DTH platforms. And Reliance, which now owns the TV 18 network, will soon own a national 4G network. Oddly, Mehta omits to mention that. On the contrary, he laments that broadcasters are not allowed to handle distribution. That may well be the law, but surely Mehta knows the reality. So why does he try to make the case for distribution?

Mehta's use of data is often suspect. Trying to establish the rapid growth of the Internet, for example, he says, "In 2013 Internet access in India overtook print to become the second-largest sub-media sector in revenue after television." Later he describes how one brand, Parle Hippo, used Twitter, to show how "social media is upending the way marketing was traditionally done".

First, in comparing Internet access to print he is comparing apples to oranges, which you don't expect of one with his background. Internet access refers to the money people pay to service providers to get on to the Internet: that's not revenue for content providers, and there is no equivalent of it in print. In advertising revenue, however, which can be compared, the PwC report of 2014 (which he cites to make his point) estimates Internet at Rs 29 billion and print at Rs 146 billion.

Second, having said how big the Internet has become and that social media is upending the old ways of doing things, he says in a later chapter that, "Internet penetration in the world's largest democracy remains abysmally low," and quotes data from the same PwC report to make the point.

Mehta's strongest invective is directed at TAM. (Disclosure: this reviewer is a member of the TAM Transparency Panel.) 8 or 10 pages of a one-sided view are peppered with loose statements like, "The trouble is that the ratings system in India has been terribly flawed for too long"; "The ratings system is so discredited that no one believes it"; and, "Senior broadcasters whisper darkly about WPP, which owns 50% of TAM, also owning a significant number of advertising agencies," betraying his bias.

Listing the issues with TAM, he describes how some years ago 500 journalists were covering the Lakmé India Fashion Week in Delhi even as there was a spate of farmer suicides in Andhra Pradesh, Maharashtra and Karnataka. How that is the fault of the ratings provider is not evident. Among the limitations he lists is that, "In a world where an average TV consumer in a big metro spends over three hours daily on her smartphone, the ratings don't provide a measure of what is happening in the digital space." Where in the world do TV ratings do that?

Speaking of digitisation, the author says that no other country's market has shifted to digital so fast. In terms of adoption of the technology, that is no doubt true; but in terms of the consumer benefiting from digitisation, certainly not. Digitisation is not merely about getting a sharper picture: until consumers are able to choose what they want to watch, and pay only for that, there is in effect no difference between digital and analogue cable. Local cable operators (LCOs) stand to be the big losers, which is why they have been stalling the change and continue to, and it is their intransigence that has prompted the government to postpone the next phase of digitisation to the end of 2015.

It's curious that Mehta skips lightly over this situation and pronounces satisfaction with its progress. Is it perhaps because big broadcasters too stand to lose from digitisation and don't want to see it progress any further? This is one subject on which broadcasters and LCOs have the same agenda.

The work he has put into the book is evident and commendable. Between his earlier *India on Television* and the present book Mehta probably knows far more than anyone else about Indian television today. Regrettably the evident inconsistencies and biases call the book into question despite its merits.

27

THE YOGI AND THE COMMISSAR

Book review

More News Is Good News: 25 Years of NDTV, Edited by Ayesha Kagal (New Delhi: HarperCollins Publishers India, 2016)

and

Network 18: The Audacious Story of a Start-up That Became a Media Empire, by Indira Kannan (New Delhi: Penguin Random House, 2016)

NDTV celebrates its 25th anniversary with *More News is Good News: Untold Stories from 25 Years of Television News;* and Network 18 marks the transition in its ownership with the unimaginatively (if correctly) titled *Network 18:*

---

[1]   First published in *thehoot.org*, Oct 2016. The title is from Arthur Koestler, *The Yogi and the Commissar* (1945). The Commissar, at the materialist end of the spectrum, uses any means necessary, while the Yogi's emphasis is on ethical purity, not on results.

The Audacious Story of a Start-up That Became a Media Empire. To be accurate, though, it is not Network 18 but its previous owners who are marking the transition.

It is interesting how true to type the two books are: the one, self-absorbed and self-satisfied; the other, racy and somewhat breathless.

The man doth protest too much

The NDTV book is high-school-year-book-meets-corporate-brochure. A collection of pieces by employees and associates recalling the wonderful times they have had, proud of and grateful for the privilege of belonging, and with an underlying note of the superiority of NDTV. High professional standards, ethical, principled. It never did anything wrong, and rarely made a mistake.

Prannoy Roy sets the tone in his opening piece. He presents NDTV as the brave victim of a corrupt environment, standing proud, bloody but unbowed, and makes a virtue of the company's poor performance in both ratings and profits.

Each of the company's three news channels – NDTV 24X7, NDTV India and NDTV Profit – was once the leader in its genre but has not been for years. Roy's contention is that this is so for two reasons: one, because NDTV has refused to prostitute itself for ratings; two, because the ratings system is not only inadequate but manipulated by unscrupulous broadcasters. To anyone who has known the news broadcasting business in India that is a familiar refrain.

It is not as if there has been just one ratings system in the country. During NDTV's life as a broadcaster there have been three. First there was TAM. When NDTV began to slide down in TAM ratings along came aMap, which showed it in a much stronger position. So while TAM was the industry standard they switched to citing aMap, slicing and dicing the data to claim leadership.

When, in time, their channels slid down in aMap too they ran a campaign citing three unnamed "major surveys across India" to claim 60% viewership among an undefined audience. Contrary to standard professional practice the ads did not detail where, when, and by whom these "major surveys" were done, or the defining parameters. Coming from a company that has its origins in psephology and counts among its brains trust Dorab Sopariwalla, the senior-most market research professional in India, it seems unlikely that this was out of ignorance or an innocent oversight.

In 2012 NDTV sued TAM's parents Nielsen and Kantar for $1.3 bn in a New York court on charges of deliberately publishing corrupt and tainted data and favouring rival channels in return for bribes. The claim included compensation for loss of revenue over a period of eight years, the amount on that account reported variously in a range from $680 million to $810 million. Calculating even at an average of Rs 50 to $1 for an amount of $700 million, that is Rs 3,500 crore or an average of over Rs 400 crore per annum in loss of revenue.

To place that claim in perspective, consolidated revenue reported in six years to March 2012 (available data), the year in which NDTV sued Nielsen *et al*, was a total of Rs 2,635 crore, or an average of Rs 439 crore a year, which is about the same as the claimed loss of revenue. In other words, NDTV claimed they lost half their potential revenue because of TAM's shenanigans. How likely is that?

In the event, the New York court dismissed the case and nothing has come of it thus far.

Now TAM and aMap (which had closed earlier) have been replaced by BARC, a ratings provider set up jointly by the industry bodies of broadcasters, advertisers and advertising agencies. BARC data for Week 40 of 2016 (1st to 7th Oct) show NDTV 24X7 with a share of 12% is fourth of five English news channels; NDTV Profit with a share of 13% is fourth of five in English business news; and NDTV India is not in the top five in Hindi news². So it would seem all ratings systems are either inadequate or manipulated.

No, wait. There's hope yet. "Another benchmark is the BARB in the UK, which just came out with their ratings that NDTV 24x7 is India's Number 1 news channel ahead of Aaj Tak and ABP," said Vikram Chandra, CEO, in an interview to *Impactonnet*. Doesn't BARB measure viewership in the UK, though, not in India? Ah, I get it. NDTV 24X7 is the *most viewed Indian news channel in the UK* – not quite *India's Number 1 news channel*, as Chandra would have us think.

The issue is not low ratings; it is that NDTV can neither improve the ratings nor live with the fact. It does not become a self-appointed moral standard bearer to constantly moan about how unfair the world is.

The Sermon on the Mount

Roy informs us that NDTV operates by what they call ("rather pompously", he admits) the "Heisenberg principle of journalism". Paraphrased, it means that for a news organisation profits and integrity are in conflict. "Almost by definition, the path to making

---

[2] Update: In week 43 of 2019 (19th to 25th Oct) neither NDTV 24X7 nor NDTV India was in the top five in its language category; and NDTV Profit was not in the top three in Business News.

profits for a news organization is littered with compromises that change the nature of journalism, often so that it can no longer be recognized as a news channel," he says, and goes on to describe three: going tabloid; fiddling the ratings; and blackmail and extortion.

NDTV, of course, does none of these reprehensible things, which is why it is not profitable.

Dismissing all Hindi news channels (except NDTV India) as tabloid, Roy contends that advertisers, advertising agencies, CEOs and marketing heads watch only English channels, "so all decisions on advertising rates and expenditure are based solely on the number of eyeballs, not on the quality of the channel, because nobody has watched any Hindi channel." Unlike the UK, he says, where a quality media vehicle gets "a much higher advertising rate per eyeball than a tabloid", in India it does not.

Again Roy conveniently, and disappointingly, ignores the facts.

BARC reports that in Week 40 of 2016 Aaj Tak generated 164.58 million impressions; Times Now, 1.34 million; and NDTV 24X7, 331,000. If advertisers were to pay all of them the same rate per 1000 impressions – as they logically should – NDTV 24X7 should earn a price per 10 seconds that is 25% of what Times Now does; and 0.2% of what Aaj Tak does. Roy knows far better than I do what kind of rates each of them gets today, but I have no doubt NDTV 24X7 gets far more than the number of impressions would warrant.

NDTV's lasting contribution to Indian broadcasting – not just news but all broadcasting – does not find a mention in the book: the infamous placement fee which financially crippled Indian broadcasters, including NDTV, and continues to.

For the uninitiated, in the old days TV distribution used analogue technology, which offered limited bandwidth. (Remember when you had no set top box and the channels showed up on your TV in a seemingly random order?) Those with top-end TV sets could receive 106 channels in theory, but fewer than 60 with reasonable (for then) clarity; and at the other end, the rank-and-file could see 11 clearly, and a total of 36 at all. Hundreds of channels competed to buy those positions simply so they could be seen and, obviously, the ones with the deepest pockets got them.

Over time the practice grew to such proportions that for many broadcasters – and certainly for news broadcasters – the placement fee became the single biggest line item in their P&L. Distribution became the first priority for the allocation of funds, ahead of content and salaries. While the biggest networks – Star, Zee,

Sun, Network 18, Sony – got into the distribution business themselves, cutting their own costs and making money to boot, all but the big five have been bleeding for years.

Digital technology will put an end to this extortionate practice, which is why the cable trade has resisted the efforts of successive governments and continues to stall digitisation in large parts of the country. That is the reason for those syrupy ads on TV sweet-talking viewers into getting a set-top box. No government can afford to arm-twist cable operators, who are politically important at the local level, so they keep pushing the digitisation deadline (now it's 31st December 2016) and cajoling viewers.

It is widely believed in the TV business that the initiator of this practice was NDTV, and there is enough anecdotal evidence to support the belief. One view is that they did that to prepare for and support the 2005 launch of NDTV Profit, going up as they were against the entrenched CNBC-TV18. But a key NDTV player of the time, who was in the thick of it then, told me years afterwards that it was earlier, to ensure the visibility of their channels prior to their IPO in April 2004.

For all his protestations, Roy goes on to accept that "on balance our news media and its 'soft power', both television and print, have been working for democracy." But, he cautions, we are hurtling towards a regulatory cliff, and that is when governments try to take control. "...the time has come once again to fight any encroachment by the government and to act before it is too late," and, later, "...any changes in the media environment must be initiated and guided by journalists, in dialogue with the judiciary, not with or by the government."

Instead of these and other similar broad statements about the way things should be, it would have been good to know what Roy and his colleagues have done about these issues. Leadership means walking the talk, not just sermonising.

Missed opportunity

The rest of the book is detail. Vishnu Som's piece *Reporting Under Fire*, reminiscent of the writing of John Simpson, stands out for actually sharing the experience: the trials and tribulations, the frustrations, the limitations, and the triumphs. That is the kind of first-person inside story you want to hear.

Barkha Dutt, who must have much to share, has only her script for a show she did to mark the tenth anniversary of her Amanpour moment, her coverage of the 1999 Kargil war. Amusingly, the script is reproduced in its entirety, complete with marginal notes and directions like these:

- "Start with an abstract close-up – a flower, a bit of a stream, and not a mountain long shot"
- "Bite – Vishal, brother of Vikram, doesn't speak very clearly – so have to see if this works"
- "Slow-mo shots of us looking at mountains together"

You're left wondering whether this is due to vanity or simply poor copy checking.

The book is a missed opportunity – for the reader, if not for NDTV. This is not just any 25-year old company. It is a company that was in the forefront of one of the biggest, most fundamental changes this country has seen, without which democracy was a joke. A couple of pieces recalling the clunky, makeshift operations of the old days are interesting and amusing, but there is regrettably little by way of insights, or of sharing what must have been the excitement – sometimes heady, sometimes tense – of pioneering private news television in the country in the teeth of paranoid regulation.

Network 18's mea culpa

If the NDTV book is about what's wrong with the rest of the world, the Network 18 book is a confessional: "a story of brilliant ideas, severe setbacks, naked aggression, spectacular victories and fatal flaws", as a cover blurb describes it. Written – very competently – by

Indira Kannan, a former Network 18 journalist, it obviously has the full approval of Raghav Bahl, who also holds the copyright to it.

The rise and fall of his empire was fraught with questionable practice, but with Network 18 now behind him Bahl has nothing to lose on that front and tells it – or lets it be told – like it is. Detractors and those in the know will inevitably have different versions of incidents, but to the outsider this is a dramatic story candidly told.

Bahl in his foreword writes with angst about losing control of Network 18. "With such enviable achievements, why do I still ask, 'Did I succeed?' Because I eventually lost control… A far more important question than, 'Did I succeed?' for any first-generation entrepreneur is, 'Why did I fail?' I can answer that for myself with hindsight candour. It was a lethal mix of hubris, unrealistic ambition fuelled by reckless debt, and the misplaced belief that I could tame any crisis."

It is creditable that up front he takes full responsibility for the denouement. There will no doubt be those who question the detail, but it is unlikely anyone would argue with Bahl's ownership of the outcome.

Adventure and misadventure

The tie-up with CNN was quite a whodunit in itself, starting with pulling it out from under NDTV's nose. Full credit is given to Haresh Chawla for the whole gutsy, brazen process from the idea to the closure, and to the surprising, little-known role of Subhash Chandra in facilitating it.

The launch and success of Colors – now the no. 3 channel in India, after Sun and Star Plus – is a story of guts and glory. NDTV Imagine (which finds no mention in the NDTV book), Real and 9X had been dismal failures. Why would there be room for yet another Hindi GEC? Colors set out to be big and pulled out the stops in content, distribution and promotion. It started with big shows, upped the ante on distribution – the broadcasting industry was agog with whispers about how much they spent – and invested heavily in advertising and promotion.

But, as I wrote elsewhere at that time, it is not enough to have the resources. It needs the risk appetite to put money, careers and reputations on the line, and then the energy to fight every single day to keep your place at the top of the league table. Chatting to Haresh Chawla when the launch of Colors was imminent, I remarked about the huge amount of money they were known to be spending. *"Paise to phir kamaalenge,"* he said. *"Izzat ka kya hoga?"*

("We'll earn the money again, but what about the loss of face if we fail?")

For all its successes Network18 lurched from crisis to crisis, most often of its own making. Having never been known to take time off, "In 2007, finally, [Bahl] would take leave – unfortunately, however, it was of his senses…"

Global Broadcast News had had a madly successful IPO, but ambition, impatience and liquidity make a deadly cocktail. Even while deep in debt, between 2009 and 2011 TV18 managed to raise Rs 1,000 crore in equity. "Stuck in a deep hole," Kannan writes,"[they] had managed to get their hands on a 1000-crore-rupee ladder…. Instead of stepping on the ladder, Raghav and his managers decided to widen the pit." And so instead of paying off their debt they blew up the money on Homeshop18, Firstpost, and a new Hindi movie channel.

That, says Bahl, was when he lost Network18. What happened later (borrowing from Reliance and their conversion of the debt into equity) was, he says, only the singing of the dirge. In his narration of the process of losing control there is no rancour, only regret. He takes full responsibility for what happened, and says Reliance did nothing more than they were entitled to within the framework of his agreement with them.

In the course of its growth from a production house to a media empire, Network18 developed a highly questionable ownership structure. Each time they launched a new channel – CNBC Awaz, CNN-IBN – they set up another company and stock analysts complained that Bahl was syphoning off value from TV18. Bahl blames "outrageous" rules regarding foreign equity, because of which the only way to get each licence was to launch another private company, off TV18's balance sheet, but equity analysts don't buy that argument.

Nikhil Vohra, CEO of a venture capital fund and one of the first analysts to follow TV18 and Indian media stocks, says the complexity and opacity of the group's structure were unwarranted. "It is completely untenable to suggest that it's the government which forced them to do what they'd done," he is quoted as saying, and that investors "just lost complete faith in what Raghav was doing", diminishing the company's ability to raise equity and forcing Bahl to support the business with debt.

Asked earlier by Shuchi Bansal of *Mint* (in an interview published as an appendix in the book) what his compulsions were to sign the Reliance deal, Bahl says, "We were in a classical debt trap. Our market cap had come down to Rs 400 crore; our debt was Rs 2,000 crore plus. So a debt to market cap ratio of 5. We would not have survived." But the debt trap was not something that happened to them: it was of their making.

Bahl does say that in terms of delivering value to shareholders the company was an 'absolute and abysmal failure', and that, "None of these analyst things would have happened if we had actually put the shareholder first." Too little, too late.

Ironically, a company built on a foundation of reporting and analysing business and the stock markets was sinking because of some of the worst practices of listed companies: opaque structures, syphoning shareholder value, and a cavalier attitude to public money. It was this attitude that led to many infractions such as buying Infomedia without due diligence, or going into huge contract negotiations without legal advice.

All credit to Bahl for letting it all hang out, for taking the responsibility, and for letting his views on many issues be presented as just that: as only his views, along with others which don't necessarily agree with his, including, on the Indian Film Company fiasco, his sister's. While that has its place, though, it doesn't detract from the rights and wrongs of what he did, by commission or by omission.

What Kannan has written, and Bahl has authorised, is much more than the biography of an entrepreneur or of a broadcasting network. It is instructive reading for any entrepreneur, and indeed for any CEO, whether owner or professional. There are of course lessons in what Bahl did – the boldness, the risk taking – but the more valuable lessons, perhaps, are in what he did not or did wrong, not just when a rookie entrepreneur but even at the height of his high-profile success. The latter is scary, and a warning to every CEO.

Different strokes...

The timing of the two books is fortuitous, enabling as it does an illuminating comparison of two leaders, of two organisations, following a path much the same in many ways and at about the same time but in two very different ways and with very different outcomes.

Interestingly, these books come hard on the heels of the publication earlier this year of the autobiography of Subhash Chandra, perhaps the original television trailblazer, from yet another background and with yet another personality and style.

For those interested in television, especially for those who have been associated with the business and have known the players, this has been a year of rich reading. But, among all of them, the Network 18 story stands out for the important messages it holds for anyone who runs a business.

Disclosure: As a news broadcasting executive the author competed with both NDTV and Network18 across genres of news. He was also associated with TAM as a member of the TAM Transparency Panel.

28

NBA VS REPUBLIC TV — THE POT CALLING THE KETTLE…?

It was inevitable. It was only a question of who would be first to pull the trigger, and when.

Two years ago, almost to the day, I raised the red flag – when BARC had just started publishing data. Asked in a Q&A with The Hoot about the watermarking technology to be deployed by BARC, I had said (in part) the problem with it is that the broadcaster controls the switch. If you're disgruntled and don't want your channel to be measured you can simply stop watermarking, and the system will not be able to read your channel[2]. That will distort the picture, and a major network doing that could hold the whole system to ransom.

Last week it happened. All English news channels turned off watermarking, and with that BARC's ability to measure and report their viewership.

---

[1] First published in *thehoot.org*, Jun 2017
[2] See page 136, *The New TV Ratings System has Drawbacks, Too*

All except Republic, that is, which was the cause of the action. The other English news broadcasters want BARC, or someone, to take action against Republic for multiple placements of the channel on distribution networks – having multiple LCNs, as it is termed.[3]

Let's rewind a bit.

"He that is without sin among you…"

As Republic was gearing up for launch the word went round in the business that it had acquired multiple LCNs on several distribution networks. Perturbed, the News Broadcasters Association (NBA), of which Republic is not a member, wrote to BARC not to report its data. NBA also complained to TRAI.

Republic went on air on Saturday, 6th May. (Saturday is a good day to launch because BARC's reporting week is Saturday-Friday and you get a full week of data from your very first week. The report for each week is published on the following Thursday.) Accordingly, data for

---

[3] A channel is meant to appear in the programme guide on your TV only once, in the genre to which it belongs, i.e., among like channels. A channel that appears more than once, in different genres, increases its chances of being viewed, because when people surf they come across it more than once, and so could increase its ratings without actually being seen more. This is a questionable practice, but not illegal.

Week 19 (6th to 12th May) was published on 18th May – and all hell broke loose.

Republic was reported to have had, in its very first week, a 51% share of viewership of English news channels. Unthinkable, and unacceptable.

Times Now, long the undisputed leader in English news, had been widely expected to crash when Arnab Goswami quit. Everyone watched keenly but week after week it remained no. 1, to the utter surprise and frustration of its competition. Then Goswami came back on the air, now as the face of Republic, and – lo! – promptly that channel appeared on top while Times Now slid to second place. Worse, the viewership of Republic was 80% higher than that of Times Now, and twice that of the next three combined. No ifs and buts: Republic was it.

Meanwhile India Today TV complained, to both BARC and TRAI, about Times Now too engaging in the same practice, of multiple LCNs. Yes, the same India Today that had done the same thing two years ago, when Headlines Today was rebranded and relaunched as India Today. According to a Chrome Data Analytics report at the time, India Today TV was on dual frequencies on each of 70 cable networks, giving it an additional 22% reach. At a cost, of course: by some estimates, 50% over its normal carriage fee.

Nor were they shy about what they had done. Ashish Bagga, CEO of India Today Group, was quoted commenting on it, and expressing his delight with the outcome in viewership and market share. Alas, the glory was short-lived: the channel was no. 1 for one week, before dropping back to its usual place in the pecking order. An expensive, if happy, week.

Times Now did not deny India Today's charge, only justified it as a "defensive manoeuvre".

BARC chose to do nothing about either complaint – NBA's against Republic or India Today's against Times Now – and for very good reason. They said they were aware of broadcasters engaging in this practice in the past too, and took the position that they "... measure viewership of channels basis their unique Watermark ID, irrespective of the platform the channel is available on or the number of instances within the platform." And, quite rightly, that "BARC India is not the regulatory body for resolving issues concerning the multiplicity of LCNs for a channel." Unexceptionable, on both counts.

In fact, BARC's policy already states, "Regulatory issues pertaining to this, if any, would lie within the domain of the Ministry of Information & Broadcasting (MIB) and/or Telecom Regulatory Authority of India (TRAI)."

Reacting to what they saw as BARC's inaction against Republic, all other English news channels stopped watermarking, thus effectively pulling out of the BARC system and rendering it unable to measure and report English news viewership at all.

Now it is reported that TRAI will conduct an enquiry. Into what, and to what end, remains to be seen.

Heads, they win; tails, we lose

Matters are now rather interestingly poised. For all the sound and fury the anchors display on their nightly shows, English news is a very tiny genre in the overall context of Indian TV: less than 0.1% of total TV viewership. Even within the news category itself all of English news is only about 8% of the leading Hindi news channel, Aaj Tak – which itself is only about 9% of the leading Hindi GEC, Star Plus.

So what does that imply for the current impasse?

The most important reason for audience measurement is for advertisers to know where to put their money. If the channel or the genre is important enough they manage without data because they cannot afford to miss the audience it delivers. That is what they did during the painful period of transition from TAM to BARC: they bought on the basis of old data.

In this case, though, it's not just the absence of current data: the whole category has been disrupted. Data up to Week 18 does not feature Republic, while data with Republic is available only for Week 19 and cannot be compared with earlier weeks. So there is, in effect, no data at all.

Nor is English news central to any advertiser's plans: it is just too tiny. There is probably not a single media plan in the country that would be disrupted in its absence. That is not to say that advertising on English news is useless: just that it's not essential. And what it adds to a media plan – frequency, impact and delivering a focused audience – it does at a relatively high cost, getting as it does 22-25% of what advertisers spend on news channels for delivering a tiny fraction of the news audience.

The affected broadcasters are caught in a cleft stick. Unless a knight in shining armour – the government, TRAI or the courts – charges in to their rescue, they have two choices: make some face-saving gesture, get back in, and risk having the Week 19 kind of data again; or stay out and risk advertisers pulling out in the absence of data. While they have acted as a subset of the NBA all of them are also members of the IBF, the biggest shareholder in BARC, and a couple of them are on its board. What they do have going for them is, of course, the clout of the news media, which can often induce matters to take an unpredictable turn.

BARC, on the other hand, is not immediately affected. The largest part of its revenue comes from broadcasters, and of about 900 TV channels in India only 6 are in English news. Their broadcasters cannot afford to pull out of BARC fully because all of them have other channels, for which they need the data.

BARC's other source of revenue is media agencies, on behalf of advertisers, who can afford not to buy English news. This means the absence of data on English news will not materially affect the value and usefulness of BARC data to its subscribers, and therefore will not affect BARC.

If TRAI does uphold the complaint against Republic and orders it to operate on a single LCN, it is highly unlikely that the broadcaster will snap to attention and comply: they are bound to fight any adverse ruling through all the appellate processes available to them. In other words, whatever Republic is doing or has done is not going to change in a hurry.

For the present, then, BARC is safe, advertisers are unaffected, and it is the English news channels that have something to think about: they got themselves into this situation and they have to dig themselves out of it.

But that is only for the present

What this standoff has done is to expose the weaknesses of the system, the better to be exploited by those better placed to do so.

First, that BARC can be held to ransom. This time it has been challenged by a small genre that does not materially affect it or its other stakeholders, but what's been done once can be done again: next time by a single broadcaster or a group of them whose absence is keenly felt and forces BARC to the negotiating table.

Second, the practice of multiple LCNs is out in the open. It's not financially viable on an on-going basis but is a useful way to get a temporary blip in ratings for the launch of a new show, for example. It distorts the data but BARC will – even if rightly – do nothing about it. So, unless there is a law or a court ruling to prevent it, it's here to stay.

The advantage of a system run by a vendor – like TAM – is that the vendor has no role in the business except to provide data. They are answerable to the industry and the survival of the system depends on their being able to keep the stakeholders satisfied.

On the other hand, the problem with an industry-owned and –driven system like BARC is that the players have interdependent relationships outside of the measurement system and have conflicting stakes in the business. Worse, in the case of BARC the ones being measured not only control the system, but also individually have the power to opt out of it at will. That cannot be a sustainable situation.

BARC as an entity is not responsible for the shenanigans of broadcasters, but those very broadcasters own 60 per cent of it and drive it. They are the plaintiff, judge and jury. Unless it finds a solution outside the judicial system in which affected parties – which would most often be the constituents of its own shareholders – can approach an objective, independent body of third-party experts, the audience measurement ecosystem can look forward to the proverbial interesting times.

29

JUSTICE DELAYED, BUT NOT DENIED

Since 2005 sports broadcasting in India has been a fraught subject. That was when the government of India made it mandatory for sports broadcasters to share with the state broadcaster, Doordarshan, the live feed of sporting events for which they had bought exclusive rights. The matter made its way through the courts from Sept 2007. In Sep 2017 the Supreme Court upheld a Delhi High Court verdict barring Doordarshan from sharing its telecast with cable operators. Putting that judgement in context...

It was over ten years in the making.

In October 2005 the Union Cabinet made it mandatory for broadcasting rights holders of major sporting events to share the signal with

---

[1] First published in *thehoot.org*, Sep 2017

Doordarshan, the (so-called) public broadcaster. For the uninitiated, here is how the system works.

An international sporting event – from a cricket series to the Olympics – is telecast in several countries, over a number of different TV channels. It is a large and complex operation. Shooting and producing the telecast of a T20 cricket match, for instance, takes about 30 cameras and a staff of 80. It is obviously neither affordable nor feasible for each of those TV channels to station their cameras and crew in the stadium or, in the case of the Olympics, in several stadiums.

That job is contracted to a single production company that, in turn, contracts with interested broadcasters, typically one in a country. The 'host broadcaster' adds commentary, graphics, and other elements, to deliver what you see on your television screen.

In a market like India multiple broadcasters vie for major events, especially of cricket, so broadcasting rights are awarded as a result of competitive bidding, with each multi-year contract running into anything from hundreds of million to over a billion dollars.

What the broadcaster buys for that kind of money is only the right to telecast the footage live and to use it for a limited period. Neither the production company nor the host broadcaster has the IPR for the actual footage: that vests with the event organiser, for instance BCCI or the IOC. Broadcasters obviously expect to earn back that cost and more from advertising and from subscription revenue from cable operators.

The argument for feed sharing was that a large number of people did not have, and could not afford, access to cable and satellite television, so could not watch cricket matches. The whole thing hinged on the idea that these were "events of national importance", and so it was the duty of the government and the public broadcaster to make it possible for the largest number of people to see them. To that end sports broadcasters were directed to share the signal with Doordarshan, which would reach those audiences.

Interestingly, in that very year, 2005, Doordarshan did on its own have the rights to a cricket series – probably the last time it did – and one day, without any prior intimation, sent bills to news channels for use of match footage in their news bulletins. The broadcasters collectively responded with a simple case. They said that if indeed these matches were events of national importance it was the public duty of the press to report on them. In the case of broadcasting that necessitated the use of footage, and the only source of footage was the host broadcaster. If, on the other hand, the matches were not events of national importance, it should not be required for other rights holders to share the signal with Doordarshan.

With that they sat down with a quiet smile and waited to be told which of the two it was. And, oh, while you're thinking about that, here is something else.

The use of footage for reporting is in any case within the definition of 'fair dealing' under Section 39 of the Copyright Act, so is perfectly legitimate. Playing off the back foot now, Doordarshan and the I&B Ministry prevailed upon the news broadcasters to accept some usage guidelines.

In 2007 Nimbus (owner of Neo Sports) paid $600 million for five-year broadcasting rights for BCCI events in India, and did not see why they should share the feed with Doordarshan. When they went to court the government immediately promulgated an ordinance and then, with remarkable speed, enacted a law.

The signal-sharing law (the Sports Broadcasting Signals Act, 2007) required that the rights holder ('host broadcaster') not merely permit Doordarshan to retransmit the signal but actually provide it with the 'clean' feed – i.e., untreated, as received from the production company, without logos, breaks, commentary, etc.

Doordarshan could then, without acknowledging the host, make the broadcast look like its own: not only put in its own logo but take its own commercial breaks, and sell advertising. In exchange – seemingly fair, in theory – it would pass on to the host broadcaster 75% of revenue earned, keeping 25% for itself.

Part of Nimbus' case was that Doordarshan did not know how to sell advertising; that if Nimbus were to sell advertising time on Doordarshan too, even their 75% share would be a great deal more, so it was an opportunity loss for them.

Nothing changed. It was only six years later, in 2013, that Star and ESPN impleaded themselves in the case.

Meanwhile Doordarshan freely misused its privilege. Given the feed to carry on its free terrestrial and DTH networks, it aired the matches on its cable and satellite channels, too. Why was that a problem? Because it is mandatory for all cable operators and satellite TV platforms like Tata Sky, *et al* to carry Doordarshan channels free of cost to Doordarshan as well as to subscribers.

This has meant that cable and DTH operators have had access to broadcast of matches through two avenues: one through the host broadcaster, at a cost; and the other through Doordarshan, free. As Uday Shankar, CEO of Star TV, put it, "...the rights holder lost money, DD did not benefit, and consumers were shafted because they were paying [the cable or DTH operator] for content which was actually free."

It was against this background that the sports broadcasters made their case. They were arguing not against sharing the signal but against Doordarshan's rampant malpractice. In 2015 the Delhi High Court ruled in their favour, and the government predictably went to the Supreme Court, which has upheld the High Court ruling.

Interestingly, to rule in their favour the court relied not on complex or arcane legal niceties but on what it called "the plain language" of Section 3 of the original law, the Sports Broadcasting Act of 2007, "which makes it clear that the obligation to share [the signal]...is to enable Prasar Bharati to transmit the same on its terrestrial and DTH networks."

So ends another long, tortuous battle. Or does it?

Welcome to Season 2

The day before the Supreme Court delivered its verdict in this matter Dish TV wrote to the Competition Commission (CCI). Ahead of the 28th August close of bidding for media rights for the IPL for 2018-22, they asked the CCI to prevent Star from acquiring those rights.

Dish TV pointed out that of 270 cricket matches played and to be played in India from 2012 to 2019 Star has broadcast rights for 191, and that is without the telecast rights for the IPL (which have thus far, from the start, been with Sony). "Once Star acquires the telecast rights for IPL as well, not only will the market share in terms of viewership of Star skyrocket but distribution platforms such as DTH and multi-system operators will have no choice but to subscribe to the Star Sports channel for cricket content," their letter reportedly said.

The Star TV network is, no doubt, the big boy of the five sports broadcasters in India, and Sony its only real competition. Star's long-time bitter rival Zee struggled with sports broadcasting for many years and finally pulled out of the genre when they sold Ten Sports to Sony. While Zee is not in it, sports broadcasting is a big money maker for Star and it is in Zee's strategic interest to choke that line of business. And Dish TV belongs to Zee.

The monopoly power that Dish TV is apprehensive about is the result of open, competitive bidding. Star TV evidently had the resources and the appetite to put big money on the table, take the risk and build a business. Is that not what entrepreneurship is about?

But Dish TV, or Zee, is not alone or unique. Reactions to the Supreme Court ruling have been interesting. *Mint* cites an unnamed top sports broadcasting executive as saying that the verdict, while fair, "perhaps strengthens the hands of sports channels too much." Let me guess: he's not from Star TV. And about Dish TV's letter, "It is fair to ask regulators to intervene."

It is the way of Indian business that we like free markets and don't want Government to interfere with business - except to restrict and restrain our competition.

For subsequent developments see p. 209, "Why Sports Broadcasting is Becoming a Lose-Lose Game"

30

THERE ARE NONE SO BLIND AS THOSE WHO WILL NOT SEE

Issues of transparency in the Advertising business: what happens and why, and the way forward. *This is a paper I presented at a conference on* The State of the Advertising Industry in India: A Critical Appraisal, *at the Institute for Studies in Industrial Development, New Delhi, 16th-17th February 2018*

When I was invited to speak at this conference I was surprised and delighted to see the subject of transparency on the agenda, and instantly chose to speak on that.

Surprised, because this was the first time I saw that subject up for discussion. Never before, in my career of over 40 years in advertising and the media, have I known it to be on the table. Delighted because, being aware of a great deal that goes on, I thought it was high time it was.

I did wonder, though. Perhaps, in the last few years that I have not been actively involved in the business, the issue of transparency has come out in the open. After all, I did serve on the TAM Transparency Panel, which was the first time I heard the T word used in the context of the Advertising business. So I asked a few people currently in the business – media agency heads, CFOs and advertisers – and the answers were the same. Had they ever had, or known of, a discussion on transparency in an industry forum? No. Did they think transparency was a serious issue? Yes.

"Something is rotten in the state of Denmark."

In the last two years the issue of transparency has come to the fore in the United States, the world's biggest advertising market by far. It did so when, in March 2015, a former media agency CEO publicly blew the lid off the industry's best-kept secret.

Speaking at a conference of the Association of National Advertisers (ANA), former Mediacom CEO Jon Mandel said financial malpractice was so common and so widespread that it caused him to leave the agency business. "[Agencies] are not transparent about their actions," he said. "They recommend or implement media that is off strategy or off target if it works for their financial gain."

This was not a conscience-stricken agency CEO, overcome with guilt and letting it all hang out. He was speaking for a Media Transparency Taskforce set up by the ANA.

Following the findings of the task force, the ANA commissioned a consulting firm, K2 Intelligence, to conduct a full, formal study. The report, titled *An Independent Study of Media Transparency in the U.S. Advertising Industry*, is in the public domain and anyone who has a role in buying or selling advertising services, space and time must read it.

The top line of the K2 report is, "There is a fundamental disconnect in the industry regarding the basic nature of the Advertiser-Agency relationship."

It goes on to say, "Neither agency professionals nor advertisers in K2's sample expressed a uniform opinion as to how their relationship should be defined, or how it actually operates. Rather, there is *substantial disagreement* both within and between these groups about *whether and when agencies are obligated to act in the best interest of their clients*." [Emphasis mine.]

Once you've said that, the rest is just detail.

The immediate response of the 4A's, the American Association of Advertising Agencies, was sadly defensive. Instead of acknowledging the problem – which everyone, most of all the 4A's, knows is real – they said the K2 report "is anonymous, one-sided and paints the entire industry with the same negative brush". That is not a fair comment because the report does have a section on "Factors enabling or contributing to the proliferation of non-transparent business practices", which actually indicts advertisers, rather than agencies. More on that later.

Comments, statements and points-of-view followed, from industry bodies as well as individuals. A year later, in April 2017, the 4A's invited Marc Pritchard, Chief Brand Officer of Procter & Gamble, to speak at its conference. He described the media supply chain as "murky at best and fraudulent at worst". But, in a statesmanlike speech, he acknowledged the role of advertisers in the unhappy situation and proceeded to lay out P&G's action plan. Across the Atlantic, in October 2017 the British government announced a full media buying review, "with transparency at heart".

The discussion has centred on the media side of the business, especially digital, and is almost entirely about financial transparency. But when we speak of transparency we must not lose sight of intellectual transparency.

Let's face it: transparency in this context is simply a euphemism for integrity. So let's call a spade a spade: the issue at stake is integrity, both intellectual and financial. Let's consider the intellectual aspect first.

Perhaps the most common, everyday intellectual compromise is data fudging. A media agency's work is founded in data, and presented in a bunch of numbers. Unless you have some understanding of the basis of those numbers you cannot ask the right questions, and can do little but accept what you are told. You can get a warm glow of accomplishment from questioning the inclusion or exclusion of a particular TV channel, but you're tinkering at the margins. The truth is deep inside.

At a media agency I was heading some years ago we were compelled to resign an important MNC account. The local client and we had a great relationship, but our global corporate parents had decided to part ways. The business was up for a pitch, and four agencies were shortlisted. The client then called me and asked us to evaluate the pitches: a great idea, since we knew the business and the background and had nothing at stake. We asked for the presentations as well as the detailed working papers. And here's what we found: in all four cases the data shown in the presentation did not entirely match what was in the working papers. Much of it was made up.

Yes, the dishonesty starts with the pitch, and there is no reason to think it stops there.

Even if it doesn't actually fudge the numbers, often an agency in a pitch does a great deal of window dressing to present recommendations that look cost-efficient above all else: prioritizing efficiency over effectiveness. In the context of media management effectiveness is buying the optimal plan at the best possible price; efficiency is buying cheap whatever you buy. Efficiency is directly measurable, in money – CPRP, CPT, Effective Rate, or whichever measure you choose – while effectiveness most often has no objective measure: it is contextual and judgmental.

This is at the client-facing level: the front office, so to speak. Behind, there is a plethora of practices, even whole organization structures, designed to get the agency *financial advantages unknown to its clients and outside the terms of its contracts* – in my book, the very definition of financial malpractice.

The most ubiquitous practice is, of course, rebating: Agency Volume Bonus, or AVB. Increasingly, client-agency contracts require the agency to pass on all discounts and benefits over and above its contracted fee or commission. But that's again one of those things that give a warm glow of satisfaction to those who create them but are meaningless in practice. It doesn't take a genius to do the paperwork such that the rebates cannot be associated with specific clients, or even show up in the agency's books.

In my agency some of our global clients had audit rights. Their auditors made surprise visits, but not one of them ever found, after inspecting our books, a single rupee going astray. Were we not taking AVB's? Of course we were. And we passed most of those rebates on to our clients, but not because we were holier-than-thou. It was only because our jobs were at risk. CEOs and CFOs were under threat of dismissal if we sat on any money that rightfully belonged to those clients. Was the global management holier-than-thou? Of course not. They didn't care what you did to deliver the financial results as long as you didn't get caught doing it.

Digital media are rarely, if ever, bought directly from the publisher. Often the media agency buys from a sister company that belongs to its holding company, or even is its own subsidiary. The agency may on paper make only the contracted commission and nothing more, but no one knows how much the selling company made. In programmatic buying there is an unknown number of links in the value chain between publisher and media agency, and several of them could belong to the agency holding company or to the agency itself. In the process, the cost to the advertiser could be anything up to fifty times what actually reaches the publisher.

Even after all that multi-layered buying with hidden margins advertisers are not sure of what they get for their money. Early last year the so-called YouTube brand safety scandal broke, when brand owners found their ads appearing with all kinds of undesirable and inappropriate content. Shocked advertisers reviewed their buying processes, and many started whitelisting sites for their ads. Procter & Gamble dropped 70% of the sites it was using.

Enough about <u>what</u> is happening. Let's talk about <u>why</u> it's happening.

There are none so blind as those who will not see

First, whatever its causes, the situation is perpetuated by ignorance, apathy and even denial.

The K2 study reports an amazing degree of ignorance and apathy. Many advertisers were unaware of the practice of rebating, and many were unaware if their agency contracts took a position on rebating. Yet others were generally aware of it, but took their agencies' word that they did not engage in the practice and left it at that. And, again, that is in the world's largest advertising market.

There is no organized information about India, but there is one interesting pointer. In 2014 EY conducted a study titled *Reality Check: Fraud, Bribery and Corruption in India's Media & Entertainment Industry*. An overwhelming 89% of respondents agreed there was an increase in the incidence of fraud in the previous two years in India as a whole; 56% agreed in relation to the M&E industry; but only 17% thought it had increased in their company.

So the incidence of fraud nearly doubled in the country and increased very substantially in my industry, but not much in my company! If the first step in solving a problem is to recognize it, we are clearly a long way away from solutions.

As ye sow, so ye shall reap

Coming back to the question, though, why do they do it? We are speaking here not of small shops and fly-by-night operators but of a 550-billion dollar global business, dominated by listed multinational holding companies, serving clients who in many cases spend tens of billions of dollars, and buying from media owners with tens of billions of dollars in advertising revenue.

K2 lays the blame squarely on advertisers:

- Pricing pressure
- Driving down agency fees, causing agencies to seek additional sources of revenue
- Shifting focus from strategy to price
- Demanding extended credit
- Lacking subject matter expertise to assess media plans or protect their interests

- Not fully exercising audit rights where they have them

In many cases the biggest advertisers want the agency to commit upfront specific rates for different media for a year, and expect it to bear any overruns. This is after they have already twisted its arm to accept an unviable fee. The agency does, but where do you – or they – think it gets the money? From rebates, arbitrage, and generally – let's use the right term – cheating clients, including the very clients to whom it has committed rates.

It is unlikely that CMOs, CFOs and even CEOs of advertisers, for many of whom advertising is one of their top two or three heads of expenditure, are unaware of what happens. If they don't know, they shouldn't be in those jobs. If they know and choose to turn a blind eye, they shouldn't be in those jobs.

Rance Crain, Editor-in-Chief of *Advertising Age*, wrote in 2015, soon after Mandel's ANA speech, "It's incredible how lethargic marketers are when it comes to policing the financial shenanigans of their agencies and the media." The reason, he says, could be to keep agency fees low.

Amazingly, Crain reports that after Mandel's sensational speech advertisers were reluctant to believe that there was fraud, and the ANA was not quite keen to move forward on the findings of the task force it had set up. "Some marketers don't care how much revenue agencies get from other sources," he says, "as long as they can keep agency fees low." It's not just that they don't know. They don't want to know.

Marketers all too often have a very limited understanding of the increasingly complex media landscape and how it works. We saw that starkly demonstrated during the formation of BARC, the Broadcast Audience Research Council.

BARC was initiated as a joint venture of the industry bodies of broadcasters, advertisers, and advertising agencies[1]. Somewhere along the line two of them – the broadcasters and the advertisers – decided they didn't need the third, the agencies: it was the advertisers' money and the broadcasters' product, so why have the middleman at the table? It didn't take long for them to realize that between them *even at the level of the industry, at the national level* – let alone of a single company – they did not have the necessary knowledge, skills, and understanding. They came back to the agencies and asked them to come back in.

If Marketing doesn't know enough about media, Finance and Procurement know even less.

---

[1] The Indian Broadcasting Foundation (IBF), the Indian Society of Advertisers (ISA), and the Advertising Agencies Association of India (AAA of I)

What they can understand is the number that shows up in the agency contract. Procurement departments are required to show how much they saved, and they can happily report the difference between what the agency asked for and what it settled for. The pity of it is they are only pinching pennies, never mind how much real money leaks out as long as the leaks are invisible.

Negotiating with one client after a new business pitch, I was asking for 2.5% commission and they were offering 2%. I pointed out that what was in contention was only 0.5% of their media budget, but 20% of my revenue, which for me was the difference between profit and loss. They didn't budge, and I declined the business.

Consider the implication of that. All the time and effort we put into the pitch was now down the drain. The client, on the other hand, now had for free the work and thinking of what in their view was the best agency in the pitch, which they could make use of while hiring the cheapest agency. What I should have done was to accept the 2% commission and make money on the side. That's the way business is done today across the world, not only in India.

If you hire and pay someone for buying cheap rather than right, that is what they will do. Agencies have the expertise you need critically but don't have. If you don't pay them fairly they will find other ways to make money – without your knowledge, but at your cost.

Over time market forces have shaped the operating model into one in which agencies have reduced commissions to patently untenable levels because that is no more their main source of revenue and profit. Thus far advertisers have turned a blind eye to it, but the underlying corruption – again, let's use the right word – is now out in the open and it is increasingly hard to pretend it doesn't exist.

Now comes the hard part

The public revelation of the state of affairs is a starting point, but it is only a potential starting point in a long, hard journey. Revelation must be followed by recognition; and only then can there be a resolution.

While the K2 report revealed their misdemeanours it was actually quite sympathetic with agencies, blaming advertisers for creating the compulsions. Ironically, neither side was happy. The agencies were immediately defensive: to say, "Yes, but you forced me into this," would be to implicitly acknowledge that there was wrongdoing, in the first place. Advertisers were slow to acknowledge the wrongdoing of the agencies, because to do so would be to accept that they were asleep at the switch: and so their complicity, even if passive.

In the last couple of years many advertisers have reviewed and renewed their contracts to plug loopholes, and many are taking digital media buying in-house. Of course, taking it in-house does not ensure that there aren't multiple layers: it only means that now you are responsible for the whole thing.

For agencies it is potentially a double whammy: they lose the extra income they were making on the side but they can't raise their commissions, which are untenable without that income. Some analysts believe the collapse of media agencies has already begun: holding companies have already begun reporting lower incomes. And some predict that digital will be followed by TV and other media buying going in-house.

Will this go away if you pay agencies more? Of course not. It has become a way of life. Personal corruption is easier to handle: this is institutionalized, industry-wide corruption. Whole corporate groups are structured around the opportunity to make earnings that are not legitimate. It will take years for new structures and new ways of doing business to come into being.

Out of evil cometh good

Maybe we are at the threshold of a renaissance of the advertising business. Maybe this churn will lead, in time, to a return to the best aspects of the past, when agencies were hired and paid for their counsel and expert knowledge.

Marc Pritchard says P&G are returning to a modern version of the full-service agency model, which was based on trust, transparency, and stable, long-term relationships.

Lead on, Pritchard, and may the world follow.

"If nothing is done about it, we estimate that by 2025 digital ad fraud will be the second income in the world after drug trafficking"

-- Stephen Loerke, CEO of the Word Federation of Advertisers, in an interview to Media Marketing (www.media-marketing.com), 22nd Aug 2018.

Excerpts from the interview:

On Ad fraud:
"In *WFA* we estimate that between 10 and 30 percent of digital media spend is actually subject to criminal activities. That is absolutely huge, when you think about it. If nothing is done about it, we estimate that by 2025 digital ad fraud will be the second income in the world after drug trafficking. So there is a huge responsibility the brands have in taking the necessary steps in order to minimize ad fraud. The ecosystem is far

too complacent today, we think, and not acting sufficiently."

On visibility:
"The average viewability in the largest markets is 50% today. So, only half of the ads you pay for are visible... Visible means being able to see an ad for 50% of its size for one second... And even with such a modest benchmark, only 50% of ads are visible."

On transparency:
"...on average, when you spend a 100 EUR, it ends up being 40 EUR for the publishers... Because, what happens in between, is often not known to the client... At times [the intermediaries] can be purchasing the same inventory and selling it back to the client without the client knowing this."

On third party verification and measurement:
"We simply can not rely on whatever a platform tells us in terms of how many views it has and what are the profiles of the people who've seen an ad. Clients need much more accountability in order to justify the type of investments they are making."

31

ONE MORE FOR THE DPOS

The broadcasting business in India has always been a face-off between broadcasters and distribution platform operators (DPOs), i.e., cable and DTH operators. It is the DPOs who have had the edge, and the TRAI as the regulator periodically stirs the muddy waters.

Broadcast networks have long refused to offer their most popular channels individually, instead bundling them with weak properties and offering bouquets at discounted prices. In March 2017 TRAI issued what is popularly referred to as the New Tariff Order, making it mandatory for broadcasters to offer channels individually (a la carte). Star India instantly challenged it in the Madras High court, as a violation of their rights

---

[1] First published in *Impact*, Nov 2018

> under the Copyright Act[2]. Star went in appeal to the Supreme Court, which in Oct 2018 dismissed the broadcaster's challenge and so upheld the New Tariff Order.

The entire Supreme Court ruling is summarized in one key sentence: "...the TRAI Act, being a statute conceived...to serve the interest of both broadcasters and consumers, must prevail...over the Copyright Act, which protects the property rights of broadcasters." The rest is detail.

That line of thinking is unexceptionable. It responds to the petitioners' argument, and states the priorities inarguably.

My argument is with the tariff order itself. I am surprised the broadcasters chose to challenge the copyright implication rather than to address its basic issues.

1. The underlying basis of the order, without which it is not implementable, is the myth that cable distribution is digital. Physically, in terms of technology, it is. But if digitization means the consumer has a choice, it is not.

---

[2] For details see, for instance, mondaq.com, *The Supreme Court Upholds TRAI's Tariff Order* (http://www.mondaq.com/india/x/755336/broadcasting+film+television+radio/The+Supreme+Court+Upholds+TRAIs+Tariff+Order)

If digitization means clear and transparent reporting, it is not.

The truth is that digitization has failed. How many distribution platform operators (DPOs) have installed subscriber management systems? How many DPOs can tell you how many subscribers they have, and what they buy? Even today a broadcaster and an MSO simply agree on a negotiated number and go on that basis. We've been through CAS and DAS, but no regulator, no government, and no law has been able to make DPOs comply. What has changed now to make them? Issuing an order without being able to ensure compliance with it is just wishful thinking.

2. Why should price regulation in content delivery apply only to broadcasting, why not to OTT as well – Netflix, Hotstar, *et al*? In fact telecom and broadcasting share a regulator: TRAI. (Broadcasting is not even in its name; telecom is.) So why does the same regulator treat the two technology platforms differently in the matter of creative content delivery to the same consumer? (I'm not suggesting price regulation in OTT: I'm questioning it in broadcasting.) I'd like to believe it is an oversight, that it did not occur to anyone, but I'm having a hard time doing that.

3. Why regulate TV prices, in the first place – in a country that has no controls on the prices of steel and cement, or of biscuits, toothpaste, toilet soap, or hundreds of other products that are used by the poor and the middle class? In mobile telephony desperate competition has driven prices to unviable levels, inevitably compromising quality of service. Who in the country doesn't suffer dropped calls? Yet the same regulator neither enforces quality of service standards nor regulates pricing in that sector. Inexplicable.

4. A pay channel in a bouquet cannot be priced at more than Rs 19/. Broadcasters can discount the *a la carte* price as much as they like, provided the discounted price is no more than Rs 19/-: the price of barely 3 days of your daily newspaper, for 24X7 content. Based on what economics?

5. The regulator in its wisdom does choose to regulate prices. The MRPs of bouquets and the *a la carte* prices single channels are declared, and let's accept that the consumer pays no more than those. But how much is the MSO actually paying for it: what is the discounted price, and therefore the MSO's margin?

6. When CAS started, in 2007, the Basic Service Tier was 30 FTA channels for Rs 80/-. Now it is 100 FTA channels for Rs 130/-: that's a 50% reduction in the prorated price per channel. Eleven years later how is that even viable? Have anyone's costs gone that way: the broadcaster's, the distributor's, or the consumer's? Anyone who thinks the distribution channels will take the inevitable hit shouldn't worry too much. It is the rare home that will settle only for the 100 FTA channels. With discounted prices and unknown subscriber numbers, there is enough and more wiggle room.

And, oh, which 100 FTA channels, of the nearly 900 in the country? 26 of the 100 mandatorily have to be DD and Parliament channels, so there are actually 74 slots available. Do you want yours to be among them? That'll cost you.

If all that seems somewhat overstated, consider this. When this case was in the Madras High Court it was the All-India Digital Cable Federation that joined it as an intervener, alongside the TRAI. Enough said.

In most businesses in India everything works in favour of the middleman, and broadcasting is no exception. Governments have come and gone; technology has changed; the structure of the broadcasting industry has changed; but, *"Plus ça change, plus c'est la même chose.* (The more things change, the more they remain the same.)

The new tariff regime came into effect on Feb 1, 2019, amid much confusion and disruption. Contrary to TRAI's contention that as a result the monthly TV bill of a household would come down, analysts are agreed that it actually went up. In

August 2019 TRAI issued a fresh consultation paper, calling for views on bouquets and bouquet pricing. Predictably, broadcasters and DPOs are ranged on opposite sides of the argument and taking shots at each other.

Pricing is not the only issue: feasibility is perhaps the bigger one. The majority of Indian TV homes – over 105 million – subscribe to cable, and cable operators do not have the back-end capability to make one channel-at-a-time changes for one subscriber at a time. So even a subscriber willing to pay the price cannot get what they want.

At the time of going to press confusion still prevails. The only positive development is that TRAI has accepted that subscribers' monthly bills have gone up instead of down. The process is on, and the broadcast sector is expected to see another disruption.

32

WHY SPORTS BROADCASTING IS BECOMING A LOSE-LOSE GAME

It surprised no one. Ever since the Supreme Court ruled, in September 2017, that Doordarshan could not share its free, mandatory-sharing feed with cable and satellite operators[2], it was widely expected that sooner or later the government would attempt to find a way around. Now, true to the script, the Ministry of Information & Broadcasting (I&B) proposes an amendment to the 10-year old Sports Broadcasting Signals Act.

Rewinding...

In October 2005 the Union Cabinet made it mandatory for broadcasting rights holders of major sporting events to share their signal with Doordarshan (DD). The argument was that as a large number of people do not have and cannot afford access to cable and satellite television, and so cannot watch "sporting events

---

[1] First published in *Business World*, Nov 2018
[2] See p. 179, Justice Delayed, but not Denied

of national importance", sports broadcasters must provide their signal to DD, to reach those audiences. Needless to say, "sporting events of national importance" was largely a euphemism for cricket matches.

In 2007 Nimbus (owner of Neo Sports) challenged the directive in court. The government immediately promulgated an ordinance and then, with remarkable speed, enacted a law. The court case dragged on, and in 2013 Star and ESPN impleaded themselves in it.

Meanwhile DD freely misused its privilege. Given the feed to carry only on its terrestrial and free DTH networks, it aired the matches on its cable and satellite channels, too. All cable and DTH operators must mandatorily carry and deliver DD channels at no cost to DD or the subscriber. They were now getting the content for free and did not have to subscribe to channels of the host broadcaster. So here's what was happening: a broadcaster who had put hundreds of millions of dollars on the table to win the broadcasting rights for an event was providing the content free to DD, which was providing it free to the distribution channels, and so to viewers.

The implication for the broadcasting rights holder is, of course, loss of viewership and consequently financial loss.

The broadcasters were arguing not against signal sharing, but against DD's malpractice. In 2015 the Delhi High Court ruled in their favour and the government went to the Supreme Court, which in Sept 2017 upheld the High Court ruling.

So the issue at stake now is not the larger question of whether and why the rights holder should give their feed, but of DD running that on its cable and satellite networks. It is pertinent, though, to step back and look it the subject in its entirety.

Why, and why the haste?
Why is the government is so anxious to make this possible, whatever it takes? The speculation in the industry is that it is under pressure from the cable lobby. It is the cable trade that stands to benefit most from the content being available free on DD, and they have historically had more clout with the government of the day than the high-profile broadcasting industry has.

The clearest evidence of that clout is their successfully stalling digitization for years, though it was in the interests of both consumers and broadcasters. One former I&B Minister candidly told me, in an informal one-to-one chat, that the government did not have the political will to confront the cable trade. On another occasion a former Chairman of the TRAI said, after a meeting with a delegation of news broadcasters, "Tomorrow we have a meeting on the same subject with cable operators. This room will be packed, there will be standing room only, and everyone will be shouting. They make themselves heard."

As this is clearly a matter of regulation, though, why is the regulator not involved in it? The system requires the government to make a reference to the TRAI, which then goes through a well-established process and gives direction. The trouble with the TRAI is that as an independent, constitutional authority it does not report to the government; and is thorough in its process, homework, and paperwork (even if you don't always agree with its opinions and conclusions). This matter was referred to it, but in March 2014 it wrote back to the Ministry that, "TRAI has to follow its established consultative process before giving its recommendations," and asked for clarifications and more information. Solution: bypass the regulator.

The rates broadcasters charge cable operators for pay channels have to be filed with the TRAI, but cable operators are free to charge consumers what they will, so they can raise their monthly subscription rates opportunistically. What came in the way of this gift to the cable trade was the existing legislation, as it categorically permits DD to transmit the shared signal only on its terrestrial and free DTH networks. Solution: amend the legislation.

This move is consistent with the government's moves to make DD's free DTH service Freedish less attractive. About a year ago the Ministry abruptly called off the auction of slots on the platform because, they said, private sector broadcasters paid only Rs 6-8 crore for a slot but earned hundreds of crore in advertising. And, they said, because all that content was available to them Freedish subscribers were not watching DD channels. What they are still getting is to watch cricket for free. Make that free content available on cable and commercial DTH, and there goes the last reason to have Freedish.

The intention of starting the process now is clearly to enable the proposed amendment to be passed into law well in time for the trade to exploit the 2019 Cricket World Cup, starting in May. The other big event scheduled around the same time is, of course, the Lok Sabha election. What is the connection between the World Cup and the elections, you ask? Join the dots and see the picture.

Substantive issues

The question of motive and timing is, admittedly, a matter largely of speculation and imputation. Keep that aside, though, and several substantive issues still remain to be addressed and answered.

No criteria or guidelines: There is no known basis to the list of "sporting events of national importance". There are no criteria or guidelines: it is simply what the Ministry says it is, with the proviso that once an event is notified it will remain on the list for four years.

What about those who don't have a TV? Accept for a moment that this is a laudable effort to serve those who cannot afford cable and satellite TV. Is the government's obligation limited to those who do have access to a TV? What about those who cannot afford one? Don't they deserve to watch sporting events of national importance?

Why a clean feed? Even without the proposed amendment the Act as it stands requires the rights holder to give DD what is called a clean feed, i.e., without graphics, commentary, and – most important – advertising. This is to enable DD to sell advertising time and earn revenue.

If you are the host broadcaster, who has paid for this content, you have two sources of revenue: advertising and subscription. Let's deal with advertising first. The content you paid for now reaches viewers of your network plus viewers of DD's network, but the advertising you carry gets only to your viewers, and that is what you get paid for. DD earns from the advertising it carries to its audiences on the back of the content it got free from you. This is revenue that should rightfully have been yours. If signal sharing is only in the public interest, to enable a larger number of people to watch the event, surely the public interest does not also require that DD should earn from it, at the cost of the rights holder.

Why cable and satellite? The amendment now proposed seeks to legitimize what has been DD's rampant malpractice for years. The inclusion of cable and commercial DTH platforms is against all logic. If the purpose of sharing the signal is to reach people who cannot afford cable and DTH, how does it even begin to make sense that DD be allowed to transmit its feed on cable and DTH? The loss of viewership is not notional or hypothetical: BARC data show that viewership on DD National or DD Sports can be as much as, and sometimes higher than, that on the channel of the rights holder.

The implication is clear. Cable and DTH operators get the event telecast for free from DD so they don't have to buy it from the rights holder; and on the other hand are free to charge customers for it. The rights holder loses; DD doesn't gain; and the customer pays for content that the cable operator has acquired for free. There is only one winner in this game, and it is not the customer.

Why the ticker? If you have been watching cricket on TV, other than on DD, after April 2018, you have seen the ticker at the bottom of the screen saying that what you are watching is available free on DD and on Freedish. This has to be the single most ridiculous requirement in this whole sorry matter. Not only are the rights holders required to give the content free to DD, they are also required to drive audiences away from themselves to DD. In what sense, by what criteria, can that be considered fair and reasonable?

If you starve the cow you won't get milk

The concept of "sporting events of national importance" can be argued for, and a case made for sharing the feed to reach a wider audience. The broadcasters have sensibly stayed away from that argument, even if they – understandably – don't like it. The EU and several countries do have regulations in that regard, but they have specified criteria to determine whether an event is covered or is exempt from it. In India as the subject of mandatory sharing has moved over the years from executive order to ordnance to law it has remained entirely without a basis, and even the proposed amendment to the act does not address that lacuna.

Even if you accept something in principle, the execution of it must be on a fair, reasonable, and equitable basis. The only way that can be so in the present instance is if the signal shared is not the clean feed but the complete feed as transmitted by the host broadcaster, which includes the advertising; if DD is limited to transmitting it only on its terrestrial and Freedish networks; and if that ridiculous ticker is done away with.

If the government continues its extortionate ways here is what will happen. Sports broadcasters, losing audiences and revenue, will have to lower their bids for broadcasting rights, in order to remain viable. Sports federations, for whom broadcasting rights are the major source of revenue, will have to make do with less, with direct consequences for the sport each of them represents. In this lose-lose game, the ultimate losers will be the sport and the viewing public whom this policy ought to serve.

In Oct 2018 the Ministry of Information and Broadcasting invited, in keeping with the mandated process, public comments on the draft of the proposed legislation, the Sports Broadcasting Signals (Mandatory Sharing with Prasar Bharati) (Amendment) Bill, 2018. *This was my submission:*

This note does not question the concept of "sporting events of national importance", or the principle of mandatory sharing of the signal with Doordarshan. It is concerned with the manner in which the principle is executed, and in particular with the implications of the proposed amendment.

My thesis is that the proposed amendment is not in the public interest, and that the losers will be the very public whom any such law and policy ought to serve.

I submit that, of all the constituents of the sports broadcasting ecosystem, the proposed amendment is mostly to the advantage of the DPOs and, most important, against the interests of subscribers, i.e., of the public at large.

Understanding the Ecosystem

The sports broadcasting ecosystem is comprised of five constituents:

- **Sports federations**, each of which administers and promotes a specific sport. The revenue with which they support their activities comes from two sources: government grants and earning from sporting events. The latter, in turn, is of three types: gate receipts, sponsorship fees, and grant of broadcasting rights.

It is only natural, and to be expected, that all events are not equal. The popular, high-profile events bring in surpluses which make it possible and viable to support, organise and manage the myriad local and state level events that enable the participation of large numbers, including school and college students, in sports.

- **Sports broadcasters**, who make it possible to take sporting events into homes across the country and enable lakhs of people, or crores in the case of cricket, to see games they could otherwise never get to see. They acquire broadcasting rights from sports federations, and take the risk of committing up front to pay an agreed sum of money, with no guarantee that they will earn it back.

To be sure, this not philanthropy, it is business, but the fact is that it is a financial risk, and it is entirely of the broadcaster: the financial interest of the sports federation concerned is secure.

- **Doordarshan,** which is the beneficiary of free content and free distribution.
- **Distribution platform operators (DPOs)** – DTH operators, MSOs and LCOs – who carry the content to homes. DTH operators and the big MSOs are corporate entities, but at the LCO level it is a highly localised, unorganised sector business.
  - *An archipelago of monopolies:* As each area is served by a single cable operator, a home anywhere in the country that wishes to subscribe to cable TV is compelled to get it from

the one LCO that serves that area. Thus while the 5 DTH operators (including DD Freedish) are subject to competition from each other and from cable, each of the estimated 60,000 LCOs is a monopolist, an island unto itself.

o *No compliance pressure:* An LCO's territory is protected, informally but effectively. As its customers have no option and it is not under the watch of any authority, it is under no pressure to deliver quality of service or to comply with any regulations including digitization, addressability and tariff orders.

o *Unknown entities, unknown numbers:* The actual number of LCOs is not known, because there is no central registering authority or record of them: they only have to submit an application to their local post office. Further, not all are compliant with even that basic requirement. Many are subcontractors of bigger LCOs, and are unknown even to the local MSO. In this environment the MSO typically does not know how many subscribers an LCO serves, which makes a mockery of any per-subscriber rate for pay channels or bouquets. In the absence of the relevant information MSO and LCO agree on a negotiated number. Similarly, up the value chain MSO and broadcaster too agree on a negotiated number.

- o *The 80/20 rule:* Of the 1,500 or so MSOs (1,469 registered as on 31.10.2017) the big few are corporate entities. The exact numbers are not available to me, but directionally it is true that the Pareto Principle, or the 80/20 rule, applies: the top few control most of the distribution in the country. The two recently acquired by Reliance, for example, control an estimated 25% of the market.

- o *Heads, I win; tails, I win:* Three of the top five broadcasting networks in the country – Zee Group, TV18 Group (Reliance) and Sun Group – own DTH platforms as well as the biggest MSOs. Consequently, these networks win the toss whichever way the coin falls. They gain whether any new measure, policy or law benefits DPOs or broadcasters. Pertinent to the present context, *none of these networks is a sports broadcaster.* Star and Sony, the two major networks that are in sports broadcasting, have no distribution interests.

- **Subscribers**, the viewing public, who have no option but to pay what is demanded and take what is given. It is over 11 years since the move to digitization and addressability started, but while digitization as technology is now widespread, the benefit of addressability is not. Subscribers still don't get to choose what they want, and still pay a flat sum of money for whatever channels they are provided.

The situation in respect of DTH is better to the extent that subscribers do get to choose from offered packages, but the transparency vis-à-vis broadcasters is still questionable.

The implications of the proposed amendment

The amendment now proposed seeks to legitimize what was Doordarshan's rampant malpractice for years. Given the feed to carry only on its terrestrial and free DTH networks, it aired the matches on its cable and satellite channels as well. Cable and DTH operators were now getting the content for free and did not have to subscribe to channels of the host broadcaster. Consequently, a broadcaster who had put hundreds of millions of dollars on the table to win the broadcasting rights for an event was providing the content free to Doordarshan, which was providing it free to the distribution channels.

When the Supreme Court in Sept 2017 upheld the 2015 ruling of the Delhi High Court, it relied not on complex legalities but on what it called "the plain language" of Section 3 of the original law, the Sports Broadcasting Act of 2007, "which makes it clear that the obligation to share [the signal]...is to enable Prasar Bharati to transmit the same on its terrestrial and DTH networks."

Since the Supreme Court has put a stop to the practice, the proposed amendment seeks to make it legal.

The inclusion of cable and commercial DTH platforms is *prima facie* against all logic. If the purpose of sharing the signal is to reach people who cannot afford cable and DTH, how does it even begin to make sense that Doordarshan be allowed to transmit its feed on cable and DTH?

For the broadcasting rights holder this means loss of viewership and consequent financial loss. The loss of viewership is not notional or hypothetical: BARC data show that viewership on DD National or DD Sports can be as much as, and sometimes higher than, that on the channel of the rights holder.

The associated financial loss arises from the hit to both streams of revenue: to distribution, because DPOs do not need to buy the content; and to advertising, because the broadcaster is unable to deliver the audiences as a substantial part of its projected audience is illegitimately diverted to Doordarshan.

The implication is simple. Broadcasters bid for broadcasting rights on the basis of some projections and expectations of revenue from distribution and advertising. When both revenue streams are hit, broadcasters will necessarily have to reduce their bids to be viable. This has a direct implication for *sports bodies, for which the grant of broadcasting rights is a major source of revenue. For Hockey India, the governing body of what is called India's national game, it is over 90% of its total income; for All-India Football Federation, over 85%; and even for BCCI, reportedly the world's richest sporting body, over 47%.*

It is obvious that broadcasters losing distribution and advertising revenue will be constrained to lower their bids, directly impacting the revenue of the sports bodies, and therefore their ability to fulfil their mandate to promote and support their designated sports in the country.

The wider implication of the proposed amendment, then, is the detrimental effect of it on the promotion of sports in India.

If the purpose of signal sharing with Doordarshan is fundamentally to help promote sports and sports-mindedness in the country, this amendment will give formal sanction to staunch the biggest single source of funds for the promotion of sports. Following from the impact on sports broadcasters and sports bodies, the biggest losers will ultimately be the public at large.

Who will benefit from the amendment?

Doordarshan is clearly a beneficiary, but it is only a collateral beneficiary. The real beneficiary of this amendment will be the DPOs. The picture is clear. Cable and DTH operators will get the event telecast for free from Doordarshan (as they were before the Supreme Court delivered its judgment), so they don't have to buy it from the rights holder; and on the other hand they are free to charge customers for it. The rights holder loses; Doordarshan doesn't gain; and the customer pays for content that the cable operator has acquired for free. Incidentally, cable and DTH operators include three of the five biggest broadcasting networks in the country – all except the two who are sports broadcasters.

The Act does need amendment, but not as proposed

The concept of "sporting events of national importance" can be argued for, and a case made for sharing the feed to reach a wider audience. Indeed, it must be noted that the sports broadcasters have not challenged the concept. But even if something is acceptable in principle the execution of it must be fair, reasonable, and equitable. To that end, **four substantive issues** in the current Act need to be addressed:

1. <u>Need for criteria and guidelines</u>:
   There is no known basis to the list of "sporting events of national importance". There are no criteria or guidelines: it is simply what the Ministry of Information and Broadcasting (MIB) says it is, from time to time. As the subject of mandatory sharing has moved over the years from executive order to ordnance to law it has remained entirely without a basis, and even the proposed amendment to the act does not address that lacuna.

   In the absence of criteria and guidelines the administration of the law is subject to the whims of the government, instances of which abound:

   - In January 2017 the MIB notified the finals and semi-final matches of the Indira Gandhi Gold Cup hockey tournament – *which had not been held for 12 years*, its last edition having been in 2005! For no stated or discernible reason the Ministry had notified a non-existent tournament. That does raise questions about the level of informed thinking behind such a notification.

   - In Nov 2018, *just two weeks* before the commencement of the tournament, the Ministry notified all matches of the

Hockey World Cup, while the original list specifies only India matches, the semi-finals and the final.

- On 4th January 2019, *just five days* before the 9th January commencement of the 2019 edition of Khelo India Youth Games, the Ministry notified the event.

Such arbitrary and *ad hoc* action cannot possibly give confidence to those who invest in the promotion of sports, or otherwise help to serve and further the intent of the law.

2. <u>Obligations of Doordarshan</u>:
   The Act does not make it mandatory for Doordarshan to telecast sporting events of national importance, which it surely must.

   In the case of tennis, Davis Cup matches featuring India figure on the list of sporting events of national importance. Since 1997 Doordarshan has had exclusive rights to telecast Davis Cup matches in India, and by the terms of the agreement All India Tennis Association (AITA) cannot approach any other broadcaster. The agreement was last renewed in January 2017 for a period of five years, yet Doordarshan was showing no signs of broadcasting the India-Italy tie scheduled in Feb 2019, and as at the time of writing the AITA has initiated legal proceedings against Doordarshan for not honouring the agreement.

If it is obligatory for a private broadcaster to share the signal because the event is of national importance, it must by the same token be obligatory for Doordarshan to telecast such events, and all the more so when it is itself the rights holder. When certain events have been designated as being of national importance, Doordarshan cannot be allowed to cherry pick from them.

3. <u>The 'clean feed' requirement:</u>
   Even without the proposed amendment the Act as it stands requires the rights holder to give Doordarshan a clean feed, i.e., without graphics, commentary, and – most important – advertising. This is to enable Doordarshan to sell advertising time and earn revenue.

   When the rights holder gives a feed to Doordarshan the content that they paid for reaches the viewers of their network plus viewers of Doordarshan, but the advertising they carry gets only to their viewers, and that is what they get paid for. Doordarshan earns from the advertising it carries to its audiences on the back of the content it got free. This is revenue that should rightfully have been that of the rights holder.

It must be remembered that the rights holder is giving the rights to Doordarshan for no consideration. If signal sharing is only in the public interest, to enable a larger number of people to watch sporting events deemed to be of national importance, the very act of broadcasting the feed serves that public interest fully. That public interest is neither further advanced by Doordarshan selling advertising and earning from it, at the cost of the rights holder; nor vitiated if it does not. It is much fairer, and certainly sufficient, for the rights holder to pay Doordarshan a broadcast fee for carrying the full feed on its designated platforms.

Further, the rights holders spend a considerable amount of money on commentators, experts, historical data, and world-class graphics, etc. For Doordarshan to spend further money doing its own (frankly, substandard) graphics, etc is a complete waste of resources. It makes far more sense for Doordarshan to simply retransmit the rights holder's full feed.

If revenue and profit are at all a consideration, chances are that Doordarshan would earn more from broadcast fee than it does from selling advertising; and do so more profitably by saving the avoidable cost it incurs in post-production of the clean feed.

It must be mentioned here that when the Act of 2007 was tabled in Parliament the then Minister for I&B said Doordarshan would use the resulting revenue to give support "to those games and sportspersons who bring medals after medals, but do not get any support from the sponsors. For instance, sportsmen of Kusti, Kabaddi, Archery and Shooting...." There is no evidence to show what, if anything, Doordarshan has done in that direction in the last eleven years.

4. The "'don't-watch-it-here' ticker obligation: From April 2018 the rights holder is required to carry a ticker to inform viewers that they can watch the same game on Doordarshan and on Freedish. In effect, not only are the rights holders required to give the content free to Doordarshan, they are also required to drive audiences away from themselves. In no sense, by no criteria, can this be considered fair and reasonable. And, again, if rights holders are required to drive audiences

away, why will they continue to bid and pay huge sums of money for rights? And if they do not do that, from where will Doordarshan get free content?

This unfair, unreasonable and ultimately self-defeating requirement must be done away with.

In sum

The amendment proposed by the Ministry is against the interests of all constituents of the sports broadcasting ecosystem except distribution platform operators. Doordarshan is only a collateral beneficiary.

Not only must the proposed amendment be dropped, the Act as it stands must be amended as described above.

Otherwise the ultimate losers will be sports, the viewing public, and the public at large whom any such law and policy ought to serve.

MANAGING

33

REMEMBERING MANI AYER

S. R. 'Mani' Ayer was Managing Director of Ogilvy & Mather for 20 years, from 1973 to when he retired in 1993. He took charge of a company on the verge of bankruptcy and left behind an outstandingly profitable one. More than that, while doing so he built a company with a strong culture, founded in a strong belief system, and always walked the talk.

He passed away on 8th February 2010, after a long illness. This was my eulogy to the person who most influenced my professional life and values.

I first met Mani Ayer in 1973. I was 21; he, not quite 38. I was a summer trainee, and he'd just relocated from Australia to take charge as Managing Director of a company in dire straits.

---

[1] First published in *exchange4media.com*, Feb 2010

When I graduated from XLRI the following summer OBM, as it was then, wasn't hiring. Subroto Sen Gupta hired me to work with him, and I started my career at Clarion-McCann. Life went on. I naturally would see, hear and read about Mani here and there.

Cut to 1985. Mani called me to his home and over several whiskies we spoke "...of shoes, and ships, and sealing wax, of cabbages – and kings". (In his typical fashion he let me know that he remembered I'd been a summer trainee at OBM.) Not a word was spoken about working at the agency. That most enjoyable evening ended with the promise to do it again, which we did. Three evenings and a dozen whiskies later we segued into discussing a job. And 12 years from that 1973 meeting I joined OBM.

Mani was a glutton for knowledge. He simply had to know. Everything. And never forgot it. When one bright-eyed young manager remarked admiringly how much Mani knew, he said. "When you fellows go to cocktail parties I stay at home and read." Quite early I learnt never to argue with him on facts, because he couldn't bear to be wrong and wouldn't back down; but, on the other hand, he always respected a cogently argued opinion even if he differed with it.

Mani gave me the most important management lesson I've ever learned, one that I hope I've practiced.

In 1989, while sending me off to Bangalore to head the Southern region for Ogilvy, he asked me to write my objectives. I defined three Key Result Areas: Profits, Product and People, in that order. He made only one change. (Or suggested, rather: that was Mani.) He said I'd got the order wrong.

"It should be Product, People, then Profits. You have to fix the product first. That is your most urgent priority, and that is what an agency is known by. Then you have to get your team together so that the product can be sustained. If you have a good product and take care of your people, the profits will take care of themselves."

He went on to tell me he didn't spend more than ten per cent of his time on financials. "Your financial performance is only an outcome of what you do. Spend your time doing that. Get yourself a good commercial partner and let him do his job." This came, by the way, from someone who not only ran perhaps the most profitable company in the industry but had brought it back from the brink of bankruptcy.

Always gentle and utterly human, Mani never presumed to tell you what you should do. He only gave you his opinion, and left you – genuinely – to do as you thought fit. And if you misfired he was there to support you, with never an I-told-you-so.

I last saw Mani in his hospital bed, about 48 hours before he passed on. He was so gratifyingly himself. His old friends and admirers will recognize him when I say that, in that critical state, no sooner had he seen me than he pointed to my shirt and said, through the oxygen mask covering his nose and mouth, "Batik. From Solo."

Thank you, Mani, for your friendship, guidance and support and for those wonderful, idyllic Ogilvy years.

R.I.P.

34

ACCOUNTABILITY IS A TWO-WAY STREET

> *If the biggest cliché in Advertising is, "I know half my advertising money is wasted..." the second is that it is a "people business". But clichés become clichés because they are basic truths. And very early in life I learnt how much of a people business Advertising is.*

A few months into my career, at Clarion-McCann in Mumbai, the agency was going through serious labour union trouble. Everyone knew something was on, but the management said nothing, and the rest spoke of it only in whispers.

One evening about twenty-five of us were called into the conference room. Subroto Sen Gupta gave us an update, and said that if pushed to

---

[1] First published in *The Smart Manager*, Jul-Aug 2011 as 'Two-way Street'

it the company would shut that office down overnight, and in its place a new agency would begin to function the following day. All clients had promised their support; all of us in the room had jobs in the new agency, and rooms were on standby at the Yacht Club.

Matters didn't come to a head, but what Sen Gupta underlined that day was that an advertising agency is nothing but a bunch of people. No building, no machinery, no technology, no proprietary knowledge or process separates one agency from another. It was the group of people in the room that made the agency what it was. The name on the door was only a label for a collection of people, and as long as they were there, there would be Clarion-McCann Mumbai.

The cynical may argue that in today's world of global oligopolies what matters is network clout. That's true up to a point. Network clout helps the agency get business: the work is still done by its people. But Advertising is not the talent magnet it once was. "No one wakes up in the morning and says, 'I want to be in advertising,'" said Michael Roth, CEO of the Interpublic Group, at the annual conference of the American Association of Advertising Agencies (4A's) in March.

So severe is the global talent crisis that the dominant motif at the 4A's was the lack of talent, not, as you would have expected, the lack of growth. On the agenda was the presentation of an Arnold Worldwide-4A's study among employees across communication disciplines.

- 30% of employees said they were likely to leave their current job within 12 months.
- They love what they do, but no one is managing their careers, so they have to help themselves.
- 96% are confident they will get a new job 'easily'.
- Most are also looking for better compensation, but compensation is not necessarily the driver for change.
- The key driver is the lack of training, growth and a visible career path, even for those with the most potential. In the absence of guidance, they develop their own sense of what is important for them.

There is little there that's new, but that shouldn't be disappointing, for research that confirms what you think is no less useful than research that challenges it. What is disappointing is that there is nothing new in the 5-point prescription proposed:

- Go back to schools to recruit;
- Promote cross-discipline training;
- New incentives, including sabbaticals, education financing, and support for families;
- 'Fix performance management'; and
- Engage employees in the conversation.

There's nothing there a standard HR text couldn't have told you, and no questions seem to have been asked about where the money will come from for more training and new incentives. More important, the solutions are only institutional, passing everything off to 'Management'.

While quite a lot can be initiated only by those who make financial and policy decisions – CEOs and the like – in an industry that depends entirely on the talent of its people, the responsibility of maintaining and nurturing that talent cannot be limited to the C-suite.

Here, then, is my five-point prescription for managing talent. Much of it can be administered by anyone who manages a team and, best of all, it costs nothing.

1. People work for people. Ask why they should work for you.

- *Are you someone they can look up to?* People want leaders who, above all, stand for something. Do you have a worldview, a belief system? Do you walk the talk?

  One of the most eminent advertising leaders in India, under whose giant shadow I worked for several years, could be utterly egoistic, temperamental and inconsiderate – but so incredibly inspiring that you ignored his trespasses.

- *Know more.* You can't know everyone's craft better than they do. But you do have to know more about consumers, markets, media, your business, and the world at large.
- *Help them succeed.* Don't compete with them. Let them enjoy their credit. They are in the game for the same reasons that you are.

2. Set standards

- *Demand work to be proud of.* Everyone can't win awards, but everyone can do good work. Show your pride in the work that deserves it.
- *Add value.* People don't come to you simply because the process requires them to. They do so because they think you will help either improve their work or facilitate its progress. Do you?

3. Some are more equal than others

- *Your people are not all equally valuable to your business.* That's the hard truth. Focus on those who make a difference: across levels and functions. Give them opportunities; take risks with them.
- *Equal opportunity, unequal reward.* Don't be afraid of giving unequal reward: or else don't expect unequal performance. But you must be fair, and be seen to be.

4. There's more to it than training programmes

- *The most valuable lessons are those your mother taught you.* In school we acquired knowledge. At home we learnt the lessons that made us who we are, developed our value systems, and shaped our ambition. The same is true at work. Classroom teaching is no substitute for good parenting.
- *Invest in those who invest in themselves.* Skill development is critical, but people must help themselves first. Self-development must be on everyone's agenda, and they must be accountable for it.
- *Advertising is about life.* The best advertising people have well-furnished minds. Books, movies, music, art, theatre, wild life, photography, travel, sport... everything is grist to the advertising mill. If resources don't permit you to do something about it, at least let it be known that you expect people to have and pursue interests outside work.
- *Be demanding of your best people.* Don't accept second best from your best. The whole team will run faster, climb higher, when the ones in the front do, not the ones in the back.

5. Talk to them

- *It's not about Facebook and Twitter.* They will find their own friends. What they need from you is someone who can give them the answers, to whom they can express their concerns. If you don't give them that, the grapevine will: and what it says will probably not be what you would have wished.

- *Accountability is a two-way street.* Your people are accountable to you, and you are to them. "Every man's first duty is to help the men under his direction," said Thomas Watson Sr, founder of IBM. Don't blame 'management': to your people you are management. If you don't want to be, get out of the way.

35

MY LIFE, IN SEVEN LESSONS

For its 7th anniversary edition Impact *magazine invited, as they usually do, several people from marketing, advertising and the media to write a piece. This time it was to be in keeping with their theme of 7. I've learnt a lot more than that, I hope, in 37 years of work. But in keeping with the '7' theme of* Impact, *here – in no particular order – are my seven big ones.*

1. Advertising is about people

No one actually needs a print ad or a TV commercial or a Facebook page or 300 GRPs (except those whose business it is to make or provide them). Advertisers spend money to induce people to do something. The half-page ad or the TV commercial or whatever is only an instrument to get them to do it.

No doubt "God is in the detail" – or the devil is, as some would have it – but don't get so caught up in the minutiae of what you do that you lose

---

[1] First published in *Impact*, Oct 2011

sight of why you your client is spending money. David Ogilvy in his *Confessions* had a delightful mythical conversation overheard on a London bus, in which one woman says to another, "I would have tried that new perfume if only they hadn't set the body copy in 9-point Garamond."

"Stop defining yourself by the *tactics* of marketing as a function, and embrace the *strategy* of marketing as a cross-enterprise idea," says Jonathan Salem Baskin to CMOs in *Advertising Age* ("Why it's so Hard for CMOs to Keep Their Jobs", 12th Sept 2011). "Own the insights and not the tools. ...understand... the drivers of engagement and subsequent action from more diverse sources. Science. Sociology. Even art."

"Read marketing books written before 1970," he goes on to say, "and history written before today's media convinced everyone that our eternal Now is utterly different from every other Then."

2. To give our best advice is our duty. To not take it is the client's prerogative.
For all the sound and fury that accompanies its work, an advertising agency only gives advice. It's the marketer who has to decide where to put the money. Your passionate recommendation to your client is only your opinion based on what you know, combined with judgement born of your experience – and your biases.

But the great thing about marketing is that there isn't one right answer. Your client is at least as entitled to their opinion as you are to yours: it's their money. And they may turn out to be right, which in marketing doesn't necessarily mean you were wrong.

3. Respect is not a right. It is earned.
"They don't respect us," is the most common lament in the Advertising business, 'they' being anyone who doesn't take you at your word. Clients don't respect agencies; Creative don't respect Account Management; Creative agencies don't respect Media agencies; Media Planners don't respect Buyers and *vice versa;* and so on round and round the mulberry bush. (The only people who don't seem to have that problem are the Creatives, but they have their own pecking order.)

If you ever feel that way about some part of your ecosystem, ask yourself what they should respect you for. What value do you add: does what you do either help them do better work or facilitate its progress?

A long-ago cartoon of unknown provenance shows a huge, imposing dam and, in the foreground, a beaver telling a rabbit, "I didn't actually build it, but it was based on my idea." Some people I show it to laugh at the beaver for claiming credit for something so clearly beyond its scope; others identify it with the role they think they play on their teams.

My advice to young people: first, know more. And not only about your specific job. Advertising is about life. The best advertising people have well-furnished minds. They have an after-hours life that is not confined to the bar or the bedroom. (It wasn't, even in the 'Mad Men' era.) Politics, economics, books, movies, music, art, theatre, wild life, photography, travel, sport... everything is grist to the Advertising mill. Have you noticed how people at the top seem to know more about more things than most people do? That's not because knowledge is a senior management perk: those who know more always knew more, and that's partly what got them where they are. Don't have the time? You'll make it, if you think it's important to.

Second, at the end of every week ask yourself what value you added. Do so by asking what difference your *absence* would have made. If you hadn't been at work all week would everything have happened exactly as it did? Was there anything that would not have happened quite as well or as smoothly as it did? If three weeks in a row the answers are 'yes' and 'no', you have something to think about.

4. The job's not over until the paperwork is done.

A media agency is a high-risk business. We incur liabilities to media owners on behalf our clients, but we are liable to pay the media whether clients pay us or not.

Consider an agency that earns 2.5% commission and operates at a 20% margin. That means every time it releases Rs 85 of media it earns Rs 2.50, and after paying for rent, salaries and other operating expenses retains Rs 0.50. If an insertion is wrongly released – wrong date or time; wrong publication or channel; wrong material; not authorised; etc – the agency is liable to pay for it but the client is not. Work out the arithmetic: that insertion will cost the agency its entire profit on Rs 14,450 of media, or 170 times the cost of that error. So every lakh of rupees of agency error costs the agency its entire profit on Rs 1.70 crore of net billing, with the corresponding impact on its ability to pay higher salaries and invest in research, knowledge and training.

Think of every release order as a post-dated cheque. There's no reason why the process and the paperwork for issuing one should be any less stringent and thorough than for issuing the other. Yet, as we know, it is not.

5. Win-win wins

We expect clients to be mindful of our interests, and to "treat us like partners". (That they don't is the other great lament of the advertising business. For that, go back to "Respect is not a right...." above. But that is not the point here.) We don't seem to think the same thing applies to media and other vendors we do business with, though, do we?

The biggest buyers can arm-twist vendors and derive value for their clients and for themselves at the cost of the vendors. That is certainly one way of doing business. But whatever your size, fair dealing brings value to all. Being a good customer means being demanding but being fair; and meeting your commitments, your side of the deal.

6. You can't cost-cut your way to profitability

Five years into my career I was hired for my first profit-centre assignment, to turn around an agency office that had been bleeding money all eight years of its existence. The office had been pared down to just Account Management, with all other functions out of Bombay, yet it continued to lose – both business and money. It was only after I joined that I was told if the office didn't break even in the following financial year – starting in three months – it would be shut down.

Faced with the prospect of that ignominy, I developed a plan to get to profitability by investing in the office to make its offering marketable. My bosses bought it, as did their bosses in the network. The office broke even in the first year and grew more than ten times in the next four, and became hugely profitable.

20-odd years later I took over an(other) operation in the red. As its nose came above the water it was put under pressure to meet impractical profitability targets. The network management was not interested in a sustainable business, only in meeting the year's numbers, impossible as that was, and proceeded to slash costs. I left. The agency – a fine professional outfit – was merged into another to make it viable.

The lesson is obvious.

7. There are easier ways to make a living, but not many that are so much fun

"Advertising is the most fun you can have with your clothes on," said Jerry Della Femina.

There are lots of ways to make a living, and in many of them you could make more money for the same effort, or make the same money for less effort than in Advertising. But I don't know too many in which you get to spend your working hours with so many intelligent, talented, fun people. Of course Advertising has its downsides, but which profession has no occupational hazards?

If you don't enjoy what you do, if Monday morning is a drag, then what Jeremy Bullmore described as "our agreeable, necessary, not vastly important, almost wholly innocuous business" is not for you. Find something else to do.

36

A MAN OF MANY PARTS

I wrote this tribute to Alyque Padamsee days after he passed away on 17th Nov 2018, but for some reason tucked it away and never had it published. Then on 14th June Lintas had a kind of homecoming, a last visit to its iconic Express Towers office before the agency moved out. That event led to a flood of memories shared among those who were there that day and those who wished they were, many featuring Alyque. And some seven months after I wrote this I resurrected it and shared it with my friends and former colleagues.

18th November. Funeral at the Worli crematorium. As the door shut on the furnace those present broke into applause.

Applause? What kind of a funeral was this?

It was Alyque Padamsee's. Who else would have evoked that spontaneous reaction? It wasn't his funeral: it was his final curtain call, as Dolly Thakore aptly said. Theatre man till the last.

He was not an advertising man who indulged in theatre. He lived and breathed theatre, and advertising to him was live theatre every day. "The art of advertising is really the art of show business," he said in his autobiography *A Double Life*. "In advertising you show off your brand rather than your characters." Every presentation was a production; every major meeting was a production: detailed and rehearsed, designed to evoke the desired response from the client.

Even a party was a production. Back when Chennai was still Madras and prohibition was for real, we had a client over for dinner. We were in a room at the Chola, just six of us – the client and his wife; Alyque; Bagu Ochane; and my wife and I – and not a drop to drink. But the party went on late into the night, because Alyque kept the conversation going. After the party he asked me, "Did you notice that I focused the whole time on the client's wife?" I did, but didn't know what I should say so I mumbled something. "Always make sure your client's wife has a good evening," he said. "He will come to your party; that's part of his job. But if she finds your parties boring she won't; and then he'll come reluctantly, if he comes at all, and leave early."

In a tribute to Alyque on CNBC TV18 the other day Piyush Pandey was asked what he thought was Alyque's biggest contribution to Advertising. He put his finger on it: "Alyque gave the advertising industry its swagger," he said.

Alyque is popularly credited with many famous advertising campaigns: among them the Charlie Chaplin films for Cherry Blossom; the Muscleman for MRF; the Lalitaji campaign that turned Surf around; and the iconic film that launched Liril. But the authors of Cherry Charlie were Pranob Ghosh and Rema Ezra; the creator of the MRF Muscleman was Hassan Taj, as Alyque himself often related; of Lalitaji, Usha Bhandarkar was. As for Liril, suffice it to say that he didn't create that either.

What Alyque did do was to foster an environment of creative ferment in which people did such work. He supported the work and harangued clients, if necessary, until they bought it; and then made each of those campaigns famous as only he could. If they are remembered thirty or forty years later, even if the brands are no longer at their zenith, they are because Alyque promoted them tirelessly.

As Creative chief of the agency he nurtured the creative product and guarded it fiercely. Sometimes he rejected a film script that a client had approved and was ready to go into production. ("Tell him Alyque said no.") And when he did that clients were not upset: they were glad to know Alyque was watching out on their behalf. No piece of work was too small to merit his attention. If he came across anything, however small, that he had loved or hated, you would know he had.

To the world outside Lintas was glamorous, and did everything in style. Inside it was always in a high state of excitement about the work. It was creative in the true sense of the word: whatever you did in Lintas, you had the opportunity and encouragement to, as Apple put it, think different. And Alyque was the star around which the Lintas solar system revolved. But you didn't resent that, because he earned that position every day.

To the end he was excited. He was interested in machine learning, and artificial intelligence, and the possibilities they hold. Raj Gupta, CEO at Lowe Lintas, summed him up when he wrote what well might be Alyque's epitaph: "He did not let the memories of his achievements become greater than his dreams."

www.ingramcontent.com/pod-product-compliance
Lightning Source LLC
Chambersburg PA
CBHW020735180526
45163CB00001B/254